THE
1999 ANNUAL:
Volume 1
Training
(The Thirty-Second Annual)

Jossey-Bass
Pfeiffer

THE
1999 ANNUAL:
Volume 1
Training

(The Thirty-Second Annual)

Jossey-Bass
Pfeiffer

San Francisco

Published by

Jossey-Bass
Pfeiffer

350 Sansome Street, 5th Floor
San Francisco, California 94104-1342
(415) 433-1740; Fax (415) 433-0499
(800) 274-4434; Fax (800) 569-0443

Visit our website at: http://www.pfeiffer.com

Printing 10   9   8   7   6   5   4   3   2   1

  This book is printed on acid-free, recycled stock that meets or exceeds the minimum GPO and EPA requirements for recycled paper.

PREFACE

Welcome to Volume 1 of the 1999 *Annual*, which is focused on training! As an avid user of the *Annuals* for over twenty years, I have watched them change and grow with the field. They have been a mainstay in my career as an educator, an in-house trainer, an external performance-improvement technologist, and most recently as a consultant and author. I depend on the *Annuals* to challenge my thinking, to increase my knowledge, to enhance my skills, and to provide practical resources for delivery of services to my customers.

Several aspects of the *Annual* series have made it a valuable publication to me and thousands of other readers. Foremost is the desire of the editorial staff to listen to its readers. In 1995 in response to the growing needs of customers, we began to publish two volumes of the *Annual*: Volume 1, Training, and Volume 2, Consulting. The materials in the training volume focus on skill building and knowledge enhancement, as well as on the professional development of trainers. The materials in the consulting volume focus on intervention techniques and organizational systems, as well as on the professional development of consultants. The "performance-improvement technologist," whose role is one of combined trainer and consultant, will find valuable resources in both volumes, which cover some of the same topics, such as "teamwork," from a different perspective. For example, if you are looking for a workshop activity that teaches the advantages of teamwork, turn to Volume 1; if you are looking for an intervention technique to improve the performance of an intact team, turn to Volume 2.

Listening to our readers lead to a practical enhancement for the 1999 *Annuals*. Starting this year, you will find more reader-friendly text. The experiential learning activities, for example, are presented to you in the less formal second person. In addition, we have maintained the personal voice that the authors of the presentation and discussion resources have given their submissions. We hope that this change makes it easier for you to use the *Annuals* and to adapt their contents for your use more quickly. We welcome other suggestions you may have to improve the quality and usefulness of the *Annuals*.

A second aspect that enhances the value of the *Annuals* is our belief that the contents of each volume must be practical and immediately useful to the professionals who read it. The content of this *Annual* has the potential to increase your professional competence and your impact on your clients, colleagues, and the field. In keeping with this, you are allowed to duplicate and modify materials for educational and training purposes, so long as the credit statement found on the copyright page is included on all copies you make. If materials are to be reproduced in publications for sale or are intended for large-scale distribution (more than one hundred copies in twelve months), *prior written permission is required*. Reproduction of material that is copyrighted by another source (as indicated in a footnote) requires written permission from the designated copyright holder.

A third aspect that reinforces the value of the *Annual* is that we solicit materials from professionals, like you, who work in the field as trainers, consultants, facilitators, educators, and performance-improvement technologists. This ensures that the materials have been tried and perfected in real-life settings, with actual participants and clients, to meet real-world needs. To this end, we encourage you to submit materials to be considered for publication in the *Annuals*. At your request we will provide a copy of the guidelines for preparing your material. We are interested in receiving experiential learning activities (group learning activities based on the five stages of the experiential learning cycle: experiencing, publishing, processing, generalizing, and applying); inventories, questionnaires, and surveys (paper-and-pencil inventories, rating scales, and other response tools); and presentation and discussion resources (articles that include theory related to practical application). Contact the Jossey-Bass/Pfeiffer Editorial Department at the address listed on the copyright page for our guidelines for contributors. We welcome your comments, ideas, and contributions.

Thank you to the dedicated people at Jossey-Bass/Pfeiffer who produced the 1999 *Annuals*: Pamela Berkman, Jamie Corcoran, Kathleen Dolan Davies, Matthew Holt, Dawn Kilgore, Arlette Ballew, Carol Nolde, Susan Rachmeler, and Rebecca Taff. Thanks also to Michele Wyman, who assisted with the developmental editing. And, most importantly, thank you to our authors, who represent the rich variety in the fields of training and consulting. In-house practitioners, consultants, and academically based professionals have once again shared the best of their work, ideas, techniques, and materials so that other professionals may benefit. Your generosity is key to the professional development of many of your peers and colleagues.

Elaine Biech
Editor
August 1998

About Jossey-Bass/Pfeiffer

Jossey-Bass/Pfeiffer is actively engaged in publishing insightful human resource development (HRD) materials. The organization has earned an international reputation as the leading source of practical resources that are immediately useful to today's consultants, trainers, facilitators, and managers in a variety of industries. All materials are designed by practicing professionals who are continually experimenting with new techniques. Thus, readers and users benefit from the fresh and thoughtful approach that underlies Jossey-Bass/Pfeiffer's experientially based materials, books, workbooks, instruments, and other learning resources and programs. This broad range of products is designed to help human resource practitioners increase individual, group, and organizational effectiveness and provide a variety of training and intervention technologies, as well as background in the field.

CONTENTS

---

*See Experiential Learning Activities Categories, p. 7, for an explanation of the numbering system.
**Topic is "cutting edge."

GENERAL INTRODUCTION
TO THE 1999 ANNUAL

The 1999 Annual: Volume 1, Training is the thirty-second volume in the *Annual* series, a collection of practical and useful materials for professionals in the broad area described as human resource development (HRD). The materials are written by and for professionals, including trainers, organization-development and organization-effectiveness consultants, performance-improvement technologists, educators, instructional designers, and others.

Each *Annual* has three main sections: *experiential learning activities; inventories, questionnaires, and surveys;* and *presentation and discussion resources.* Each published submission is classified in one of the following categories: Individual Development, Communication, Problem Solving, Groups, Teams, Consulting and Facilitating, Leadership, and Organizations. Within each category, pieces are further classified into logical subcategories, which are identified in the introductions to the three sections.

The last category, Organizations, is making its debut in the 1999 *Annual.* This addition reflects the changing nature of the field, as professionals take on more and more responsibilities in their organizations or as consulting professionals to organizations. The more widely accepted role of performance-improvement technologist brings with it more broadly defined responsibilities, often more "organizational" in nature. In addition, after four years of publishing a separate consulting volume, the need to incorporate the broader Organization category in the *Annual* series has become self-evident. We encourage you to broaden your perspective to include this category as you consider submitting material for future *Annuals.*

You will also find a new subcategory in the 1999 *Annual:* "Technology." Much has changed for the HRD professional in recent years, and technology has lead much of that change. Given the important role technology plays, we will continue to publish material that relates technology to the HRD field and how the HRD professional can use technology as a tool.

Another addition to the 1999 *Annual* is the identification of "cutting edge" topics. This designation highlights topics that present information, concepts, tools, or perspectives that may be recent additions to the profession or that have not previously appeared in the *Annual.*

The series continues to provide an opportunity for HRD professionals who wish to share their experiences, their viewpoints, and their processes with their colleagues. To that end, Jossey-Bass/Pfeiffer publishes guidelines for potential authors. These guidelines are available from the Pfeiffer editorial department at Jossey-Bass Inc., Publishers, in San Francisco, California.

Materials are selected for the *Annuals* based on the quality of the ideas, applicability to real-world concerns, relevance to current HRD issues, clarity of presentation, and ability to enhance our readers' professional development. In addition, we choose experiential learning activities that will create a high degree of enthusiasm among the participants and add enjoyment to the learning process. As in the past several years, the contents of each *Annual* span a wide range of subject matter, reflecting the range of interests of our readers.

Our contributor list includes a wide selection of experts in the field: in-house practitioners, consultants, and academically based professionals. A list of contributors to the *Annual* can be found at the end of the volume, including their names, affiliations, addresses, telephone numbers, facsimile numbers, and e-mail addresses. Readers will find this list useful if they wish to locate the authors of specific pieces for feedback, comments, or questions. Further information is presented in a brief biographical sketch of each contributor that appears at the conclusion of each article. We publish this information to encourage "networking," which continues to be a valuable mainstay in the field of human resource development.

We are pleased with the high quality of material that is submitted for publication each year and often regret that we have page limitations. In addition, just as we cannot publish every manuscript we receive, you may find that not all published works are equally useful to you. Therefore, we encourage and invite ideas, materials, and suggestions that will help us to make subsequent *Annuals* as useful as possible to all of our readers.

Introduction
to the Experiential Learning Activities Section

Experiential learning activities ensure that lasting learning occurs and should be selected with a specific learning objective in mind. Although the experiential learning activities presented here all vary in goals, group size, time required and process[1], they all incorporate one important element: questions that facilitate the learning. This final discussion, lead by the facilitator, assists the participants to process the activity, to internalize the learning, and to relate it to their day-to-day situations. It is this element that creates the unique experience and learning opportunity that only an experiential learning activity can bring to the group process.

Readers have used the *Annuals'* experiential learning activities for years to enhance their training and consulting events. Each learning experience is complete and includes all lecturettes, handout content, and other written material necessary to facilitate the activity. In addition each includes variations of the design that the facilitator might find useful. Although the activity as written may not fit perfectly with your objective, within your time frame, or to your group size, we encourage you to use these variations as well as your own variations. Should you wish to look beyond this volume for additional experiential learning activities, we encourage you to peruse the "Experiential Learning Activities Categories" chart that immediately follows this introduction.

The 1999 Annual: Volume 1, Training includes fourteen activities, in the following categories:

Individual Development: Diversity

617. Expanding the Scope of Diversity Programs: A New Model
by Julie O'Mara

---

[1]It would be redundant to print here a caveat for the use of experiential learning activities, but HRD professionals who are not experienced in the use of this training technology are strongly urged to read the "Introduction" to the *Reference Guide to Handbooks and Annuals* (1997 Edition). This article presents the theory behind the experiential-learning cycle and explains the necessity of adequately completing each phase of the cycle to allow effective learning to occur.

Leadership: Styles

630. Rope-a-Leader: Experiencing the Emergence of Leadership
by John W. Peterson and Sherry R. Mills

Other activities that address goals in these and other categories can be located by using the "Experiential Learning Activities Categories" chart that follows, or by using our comprehensive *Reference Guide to Handbooks and Annuals*. This book, which is updated regularly, indexes all of the *Annuals* and all of the *Handbooks of Structured Experiences* that we have published to date. With each revision, the *Reference Guide* becomes a complete, up-to-date, and easy-to-use resource for selecting appropriate materials from all of the *Annuals* and *Handbooks*.

Experiential Learning Activities Categories

		Vol.	Page
INDIVIDUAL DEVELOPMENT			
Sensory Awareness			
Feelings & Defenses (56)		III	31
Lemons (71)		III	94
Growth & Name Fantasy (85)		'72	59
Group Exploration (119)		IV	92
Relaxation & Perceptual Awareness (136)		'74	84
T'ai Chi Chuan (199)		VI	10
Roles Impact Feelings (214)		VI	102
Projections (300)		VIII	30
Mastering the Deadline Demon (593)		'98–1	9
Self-Disclosure			
Johari Window (13)		I	65
Graphics (20)		I	88
Personal Journal (74)		III	109
Make Your Own Bag (90)		'73	13
Growth Cards (109)		IV	30
Expressing Anger (122)		IV	104
Stretching (123)		IV	107
Forced-Choice Identity (129)		'74	20
Boasting (181)		'76	49
The Other You (182)		'76	51
Praise (306)		VIII	61
Introjection (321)		'82	29
Personality Traits (349)		IX	158
Understanding the Need for Approval (438)		'88	21
The Golden Egg Award (448)		'88	89
Adventures at Work (521)		'95–1	9
That's Me (522)		'95–1	17
Knowledge Is Power (631)		'99–2	13
Sex Roles			
Polarization (62)		III	57
Sex-Role Stereotyping (95)		'73	26
Sex-Role Attributes (184)		'76	63
Who Gets Hired? (215)		VI	106
Sexual Assessment (226)		'78	36
Alpha II (248)		VII	19
Sexual Values (249)		VII	24
Sex-Role Attitudes (258)		VII	85
Sexual Values in Organizations (268)		VII	146

		Vol.	Page
Sexual Attraction (272)		'80	26
Sexism in Advertisements (305)		VIII	58
The Promotion (362)		IX	152
Raising Elizabeth (415)		'86	21
The Problem with Men/Women Is . . . (437)		'88	9
The Girl and the Sailor (450)		'89	17
Tina Carlan (466)		'90	45
Diversity			
Status-Interaction Study (41)		II	85
Peer Perceptions (58)		III	41
Discrimination (63)		III	62
Traditional American Values (94)		'73	23
Growth Group Values (113)		IV	45
The In-Group (124)		IV	112
Leadership Characteristics (127)		'74	13
Group Composition (172)		V	139
Headbands (203)		VI	25
Sherlock (213)		VI	92
Negotiating Differences (217)		VI	114
Young/Old Woman (227)		'78	40
Pygmalion (229)		'78	51
Race from Outer Space (239)		'79	38
Prejudice (247)		VII	15
Physical Characteristics (262)		VII	108
Whom To Choose (267)		VII	141
Data Survey (292)		'81	57
Lifeline (298)		VIII	21
Four Cultures (338)		'83	72
All Iowans Are Naive (344)		IX	14
AIRSOPAC (364)		IX	172
Doctor, Lawyer, Indian Chief (427)		'87	21
Life Raft (462)		'90	17
Zenoland (492)		'92	69
First Impressions (509)		'94	9
Parole Board (510)		'94	17
Fourteen Dimensions (557)		'96–2	9
Adoption (570)		'97–1	9
Globalization (570)		'97–1	19
Generational Pyramids (571)		'97–1	33

		Vol.	Page
People with Disabilities (594)		'98–1	15
Expanding the Scope of Diversity Programs (617)		'99–1	13
Life/Career Planning			
Life Planning (46)		II	101
Banners (233)		'79	9
Wants Bombardment (261)		VII	105
Career Renewal (332)		'83	27
Life Assessment and Planning (378)		'85	15
Work-Needs Assessment (393)		X	31
The Ego-Radius Model (394)		X	41
Dropping Out (414)		'86	15
Roles (416)		'86	27
Creating Ideal Personal Futures (439)		'88	31
Pie in the Sky (461)		'90	9
What's in It for Me? (463)		'90	21
Affirmations (473)		'91	9
Supporting Cast (486)		'92	15
Career Visioning (498)		'93	13
The Hand You're Dealt (523)		'95–1	23
Living Our Values (548)		'96–1	25
Career Roads (549)		'96–1	35
Collaborating for Success (572)		'97–1	45
High Jump (573)		'97–1	57
Issues, Trends, and Goals (595)		'98–1	21
Bouncing Back (596)		'98–1	35
Work Activities (597)		'98–1	43
COMMUNICATION			
Awareness			
One-Way, Two-Way (4)		I	13
Think-Feel (65)		III	70
Ball Game (108)		IV	27
Re-Owning (128)		'74	18
Helping Relationships (152)		V	13
Babel (153)		V	16
Blindfolds (175)		'76	13
Letter Exchange (190)		'77	28

617. Expanding the Scope of Diversity Programs: A New Model

Goals

- To help participants see the relationships among diversity in their company's workforce, its marketplace, and its structures.

- To show how broadly diversity can be defined.

- To enable participants to understand that diversity is about more than race and gender.

- To help participants think of new ways to handle issues of workplace diversity in the future.

Group Size

As many as thirty participants from organizations involved in diversity interventions currently or considering them in the future.

Time Required

Approximately one hour and thirty minutes.

Materials

- A wall chart or an overhead transparency, drawn in advance of the workshop, of the three-circle model of Expanding the Scope of Diversity Programs: Workforce, Marketplace, Structures.

- One copy of the Expanding the Scope of Diversity Programs Reading Sheet for each participant.

- A flip chart and several colors of felt-tipped markers for each subgroup.

- A flip chart and several colors of felt-tipped markers for the facilitator.

Physical Setting

A room with plenty of space so that subgroups do not disturb one another as they work. A round table and moveable chairs are ideal—but not essential—for each subgroup.

Process

1. Announce the goals of the activity.

2. Using the wall chart or transparency of the model, prepared in advance, give a lecturette based on the Expanding the Scope of Diversity Programs Reading Sheet. Give copies of the sheet to each participant for future reference. (Ten minutes.)

3. Ask participants to form subgroups of equal size with at least five persons each. If possible, participants should be from different departments or units of the same organization. Tell each subgroup to convene at a different table or to pull their chairs into a circle. Give each subgroup a flip chart and several different colors of felt-tipped markers. (Five minutes.)

4. Leave the model posted. Explain the task, writing it on a flip chart at the same time, as follows (*Note:* These instructions can also be prepared in advance):

   - Appoint one or two members to record discussion highlights on the flip chart and to be the spokespersons for your group.

   - Recalling the lecturette and referring to the handout as needed, find two examples that are relevant for your department(s) for each of the overlapping categories on the model: (1) the workforce and the marketplace; (2) the marketplace and structures; and (3) structures and the workforce.

   - What intervention could your training or HR department make in your organization based on this model?

5. Explain that the subgroups will have fifteen minutes to complete this task. Monitor their work, and let the subgroups know when only a few minutes remain. (Twenty-five minutes.)

6. After fifteen minutes, call time, reconvene the total group, and ask the spokespersons to take turns presenting the highlights of their discussions, limiting their presentations to four minutes or under. After each spokesperson reports, ask for brief questions or comments from the other subgroups. (Thirty minutes.)

7. Lead a concluding discussion based on the following questions, summarizing their answers on a flip chart:

- Have you gained any insights about how company workforce, marketplace, and structures interact? If so, what are they? How can you use your new knowledge on the job?

- What means will you use to remember this new approach to diversity at work? What might hinder your thinking in a new way back on the job? How can you overcome thinking in the old way?

(Twenty minutes.)

Variations

- As a first step, groups may list problems or missed opportunities that are faced by their organization, then create examples of how workforce, marketplace, and structural interventions could have been used to address those problems and missed opportunities.

- Assign subgroups only one category each, then discuss in the large group. This will save some time.

- After the discussion, reassemble the subgroups and ask them to determine the next steps they should take to cause each of their examples to be enhanced or enacted by the organization when they return to work.

Submitted by Julie O'Mara.

Julie O'Mara, a consultant specializing in leadership and diversity, uses an organization development, systems-change approach in her work. She is co-author of Managing Workforce 2000: Gaining the Diversity Advantage *(Jossey-Bass) and author of* Diversity Activities and Training Designs *(Jossey-Bass/Pfeiffer). She is past president of the American Society for Training and Development and the recipient of several awards, including Ben Bostic Trainer of the Year (1995) from the Multicultural Network and ASTD's Valuing Differences Award (1997) for work with the Royal Bank of Canada.*

EXPANDING THE SCOPE OF DIVERSITY
PROGRAMS READING SHEET

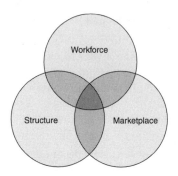

**Expanding the Scope of Diversity Programs:
Workforce, Marketplace, Structures**

Most organizations today continue to define diversity in the context of the workforce and in some version of the primary and secondary dimensions of diversity, which Marilyn Loden and Judy Rosener (1991) described in *Workforce America.*

In the United States and most Western cultures, *primary* dimensions of diversity are considered to be age, race, ethnicity, gender, physical abilities/ qualities, and sexual/affectional orientation. These dimensions represent the core of individual identities, exert an important impact on our early socialization, and have an ongoing impact throughout our lives. *Secondary* dimensions we usually consider to be those that can be changed. They include, but are not limited to, geographic location, educational background, work experience, and marital and parental status. In other cultures, the content of the primary and secondary dimensions may be different, but the concept of primary and secondary dimensions remains. It is important to note that everyone is included in these dimensions.

Roosevelt Thomas' (1991) book, *Beyond Race and Gender,* one of the landmark books on diversity, has helped to expand our thinking about the topic. The title is especially meaningful—"beyond race and gender." Thomas believes that for diversity efforts to be successful in organizations, it is helpful to expand our thinking to include diversity in the marketplace and in our organizational structures—and to think not only of the increasingly diverse workforce.

Today organizations on the leading edge are expanding their thinking about diversity, thinking not only of the primary dimensions in the context of the workforce, but about how differences and similarities among people impact the marketplace and how our organizational structures increase or decrease feelings of inclusion, which can impact how decisions are made. They are finding that this expanded definition and approach increase the interest and excitement of managers and employees alike, and thereby increase the desire of people in organizations to address the challenges and opportunities inherent in diversity. Descriptions of the three dimensions of diversity follow.

Workforce diversity includes challenges and opportunities that exist between the current and future workforce: attracting and retaining individuals; assuring equity in performance management, promotions, and benefits; and reducing barriers to doing work.

Marketplace diversity includes challenges and opportunities that exist because the marketplace is diverse. Strategies to increase marketplace diversity include market segmenting, expanding to global markets, and a variety of delivery channels and advertising approaches. Serving the marketplace with sensitivity to diversity is a key strategy for success in today's business world.

Structural diversity refers to how the structures of organizations can result in inclusion or exclusion. Structures can help or hinder individuals and groups interacting with one another to accomplish work. This component is the most unusual to be included under a banner of diversity. Jack Welch, CEO of General Electric, speaks of a boundaryless organization. A boundaryless organization operates swiftly and with little territorial conflict and ownership. Attention to structural diversity means that cultures and systems are blended across levels and functions, and between units, departments, parent organizations and subsidiaries, merged organizations or units, and work teams.

These three areas—workforce, marketplace, and structures—overlap. As the model above suggests, for diversity work to be successful in organizations, interventions must be performed in all three areas.

Here are some examples of how these three areas are related:

- *The Workforce and Marketplace:* Product developers must have knowledge about people with disabilities to assure that new products can be used by this growing segment of the marketplace. Possible interventions here include hiring product developers who have disabilities or who have experience designing for people with disabilities, learning to increase knowledge and understanding of how people with disabilities will use the products, and conducting focus groups and field testing with people with disabilities participating.

- *The Marketplace and Structures:* To assure that customers are served better, organizational units must work swiftly and collaboratively. Whereas in the past they may have moved new ideas and decisions through the hierarchy level by level, they now may need to put information on the company intranet for people at various levels and in various units to comment simultaneously.

- *Structures and the Workforce:* To serve the organization well, human resource professionals must know the business of the organization, as well as human resource strategies and technology. Possible interventions include cross-level, cross-functional teams of line and staff managers to address outsourcing, recruiting, or downsizing. Another intervention may be to redesign jobs so that human resource professionals are part of a line rather than a staff organization.

- *Workforce, Marketplace, and Structures:* Examples of interventions that touch on all three components include:

  - Changing recruiting strategies and process to increase the number of persons who speak the language of a growing segment of the identified customer base.

  - Creating teams comprised of customers, suppliers, and employees to improve products and processes.

  - Using institutional advertising to increase the number of recent college graduates who can bring cutting edge thinking to various units.

The organizational diversity model can help expand an organization's thinking about diversity, moving it not only beyond race and gender, but beyond the workforce to the marketplace and organizational structures.

References

Loden, M., & Rosener, J. (1991). *Workforce America.* Burr Ridge, IL: Irwin Professional.

Thomas, R. (1991). *Beyond race and gender.* New York: AMACOM.

618. The M&M® Game: Learning To Resolve Conflict

Goals

- To observe individual and team conflict resolution when resources are unequal.

- To acquaint the participants with conflict-resolution strategies.

- To offer the participants an opportunity to experience and compare the effects and outcomes from different conflict-resolution strategies.

Group Size

Twenty to thirty participants, as written, but could be played by any number.

Time Required

Approximately one hour.

Materials

- An M&M® Game Conflict-Resolution Lecturette Sheet for the facilitator.
- An M&M® Game Keys to Processing Sheet for the facilitator.
- One M&M® Game Goals and Rules overhead transparency.
- A one-pound package of M&M®s plain candy.
- One copy of the M&M® Game Conflict-Resolution Paired Discussion Sheet for each participant.
- A pencil or pen and paper for each participant.
- An overhead projector and blank transparencies.
- A flip chart and markers.
- An accurate timer or watch.

Physical Setting

A room large enough so that all participants can move freely around the room while negotiating conflict-resolution strategies with one another.

Process

1. Prior to the session, read the M&M® Conflict-Resolution Lecturette Sheet and develop a lecturette to present to participants. Make a copy of the M&M® Game Goals and Rules on an overhead transparency or on a flip chart, and read through the M&M® Game Keys to Processing Sheet to be sure you understand the nuances of the game and are prepared for the ensuing discussion.

2. After participants are seated, pass the bag of M&M®s around and instruct them to take three M&M®s each, but not to eat them. While the participants are passing the bag, introduce the topic of conflict resolution by giving a lecturette on the topic of conflict resolution from the M&M® Game Conflict-Resolution Lecturette Sheet.

3. Ask the following questions to encourage discussion, writing their answers on the flip chart:

   ■ How would you define conflict? *(Suggested response:* A state of disharmony between seemingly incompatible ideas or interests.)

   ■ What does the word "resolution" conjure up in your mind? *(Suggested response:* A course of action to solve a problem, a solution.)

   Be sure to bring out that each person has a different style of dealing with conflict. Remind participants that all styles are appropriate to use at various times.

4. Display the M&M® Game Goals and Rules overhead transparency or flip chart and explain the game. Answer questions, but do not discuss strategy. Make sure that no one starts until you say, "Go!" Tell participants that you will be the time keeper, and that they will have five minutes to complete the game. Tell them to "go." (Ten minutes.)

5. Give a one-minute warning. After five minutes, stop the game. Ask participants to return to their seats.

6. Use the following questions to process the activity.

   ■ What happened during the game?

   ■ What techniques did you use or see others use to acquire M&M®s?

- Did you consider joining forces with another participant? Why or why not?

- How might your strategy have changed if you had formed teams?

- How did you interpret the goal? How did the words "as possible" affect your working toward the goal?

- Did you try bargaining? Did it work? Why or why not?

- What would have been the result if everyone had collaborated? Would that have been a better result? Why or why not?

(Fifteen minutes.)

7. Give a copy of the M&M® Game Conflict-Resolution Paired Discussion Sheet, paper, and a pen or pencil to each participant. Have them form pairs and find a quiet location to complete the questions together. (Twenty minutes.)

8. When the pairs have finished, reconvene the large group and conclude with a discussion summarizing the activity, using these questions:

- What did you learn about conflict and conflict resolution from doing this activity?

- If you were to do this activity again, what would you do differently?

- What did you learn from this activity about how you handle conflict?

- How might you handle conflict differently in the future?

(Ten minutes.)

Variations

- This activity can be adapted to acquaint the participants with using bases of power.

- Instead of the discussions in pairs, role plays could be developed.

Suggested Readings

Blake, R.B., & Mouton, J.S. (1970). The fifth achievement. In *The Journal of Applied Behavioral Science, 6*(4), 413–426.

Fisher R., & Ury, W. (1981). *Getting to yes: Negotiating agreement without giving in.* New York: Penguin.

French, J.R.P., Jr., & Kruglaski, W. (1975). The bases of social power. In D. Cartwright (Ed.), *Studies in social power.* Ann Arbor, MI: Institute for Social Research.

Hall, J. (1969). *Conflict management survey*. Houston, TX: Teleometrics.

Hersey, P., Blanchard, K.H., & Natemeyer, W.E. (1979). *Situational leadership: Perception and the impact of power*. Escondido, CA: Leadership Studies.

Karp, H.B., (1985). *Personal power: An unorthodox guide to success*. New York: AMACOM.

Mauer, R. (1996). *Beyond the wall of resistance: Unconventional strategies that build support for change*. Austin, TX: Bard Books.

Raven, B.H., & Kruglanski, W. (1975). Conflict and power. In P.G. Swingle (Ed.), *The structure of conflict*. New York: Academic Press.

Robert, M. (1982). Conflict management style survey. In J.W. Pfeiffer & L.D. Goodstein (Eds.), *The 1982 annual for facilitators, trainers, and consultants*. San Francisco, CA: Jossey-Bass/Pfeiffer.

Thomas, K.W. (1967). Conflict and conflict management. In M. Dunnette (Ed.), *Handbook of industrial and organizational psychology* (Vol. 2). New York: John Wiley.

Thomas, K.W., & Kilmann, R.H. (1974). *Thomas-Kilmann conflict mode instrument*. Tuxedo, NY: XICOM, Inc.

Wiley, G.E. (1973). Win/lose situations. In J.E. Jones & J.W. Pfeiffer (Eds.), *The 1973 annual handbook for group facilitators*. San Francisco, CA: Jossey-Bass/Pfeiffer.

Submitted by Gerald V. Miller.

Gerald V. Miller, Ph.D., *is president of Gerald V. Miller Associates, a management consulting and training firm. He consults with a variety of Fortune 500 companies and public organizations in the areas of leadership development and managing change. He has over twenty years' experience as a specialist in management, organization, and human resource development. He blends organizational and leadership assessment and training with productivity improvement strategies so that his customers see a quantitative and qualitative return on their investment.*

M&M® GAME CONFLICT-RESOLUTION LECTURETTE SHEET

Instructions: Use the information below as a basis for introducing the topic of conflict resolution. You may give a lecturette directly from this sheet or add whatever material you desire.

Conflict

Conflict is one of the more potent of human interactions. It can either facilitate growth or bring harm to the people involved. Perhaps because of its potency, "conflict" has become a loaded word, carrying many negative connotations. There are many popular misconceptions of the meaning and purpose of conflict. People think of conflict as negative, but it may actually be positive and enhance one's strength, clarify one's purpose, or encourage action.

Conflict is a daily reality. Whether at home or at work, our needs and values continually and invariably come into opposition with those of others. Some conflicts are relatively minor, easy to handle, or capable of being overlooked. Others, however, require a strategy for successful resolution to avoid lasting enmity.

The ability to resolve conflict successfully is probably one of the most important skills that you can possess. Yet there are few formal opportunities to learn conflict-resolution skills. This experiential learning activity provides you with such an opportunity.

Like any other human skill, conflict resolution can be taught; like other skills, it consists of a number of important subskills, each separate and yet interdependent. These skills must be assimilated at the cognitive level. Ask yourself: Do I understand how conflict can be resolved? And also at the behavioral level: Can I resolve specific conflicts?

M&M® GAME KEYS TO PROCESSING SHEET

Processing the Game

1. A key point that will come up is that participants will not think in terms of forming teams to achieve their goals, but rather in terms of competition—leading to conflict. There will most likely be an assumption that the word "you" is singular, rather than plural. Be sure to discuss this point (making assumptions) thoroughly.

2. Another concept that is hard for participants to understand is that simply having the most of a certain color does not cause them to win. The goal is to "collect as many of the same color as possible." Therefore, if an individual or team acquires four blue M&M®s and there are only four blue M&M®s available during the game, then they have met the goal. Brown is the predominate color in a bag of M&M®s. Individuals or teams collecting brown candies generally believe that they have won because they have the highest number. *This is only true if they have all the brown M&M®s that were out during the game.* This calls for a discussion of clarifying rules prior to forging ahead with a game.

3. Participants should also learn that when individuals or teams primarily use compromise or bargaining in this game, they cannot win because of the unequal distribution of the colors of M&M®s. With bargaining, one eventually has nothing to trade, if he or she does not possess the color the other person needs. The game can be won by an individual, but because of limited time and variation in color, one person would probably have to use sheer force of will to win.

4. Collaboration and team effort are needed to "win." Teaming up on a particular color will ensure a win-win result. If everyone chooses collaboration to resolve the conflict, it is possible for many teams to win. It is also possible for the large group to collaborate, that is, to agree to share all the M&M®s and simply divide them by color category.

5. As stated above, it is possible for one individual to win the game by going for a particular color and using strong force of will on the other group members. However, that strategy will only work in the short term, as others will resent such behavior. The conflict will not be resolved, but probably will escalate.

M&M® GAME GOALS AND RULES

Goal:

In the next five minutes you are to collect as many of the same color M&M®s as possible.

Rules:

1. Do not start until I say, "Go!"

2. How you achieve the goal is up to you.

3. Do no bodily harm!

4. You may only use the M&M®s that are out at this time.

M&M® Game Conflict-Resolution Paired Discussion Sheet

Instructions: Spend twenty minutes with your partner discussing the following and writing down your answers:

1. List words that describe how you deal with conflict, for example, collaborate, submit, accommodate others' needs, persuade, force, fight, flee, compete, avoid, bargain, compromise:

   _____

   _____

2. What do these words tell you about your conflict-resolution style?

   _____

   _____

3. What insights or learnings about your conflict-resolution style did you have during the activity?

   _____

   _____

4. Which of these insights is potentially the most useful to you in the future? Why?

   _____

   _____

5. As a result of your key discoveries, what will you:

   ■ Continue doing?

   _____

   _____

   ■ Start doing?

   _____

   _____

   ■ Stop doing?

   _____

   _____

619. VIRTUAL SCAVENGER HUNT: LEARNING TO USE THE WORLD WIDE WEB

Goals

- To help participants learn the skills needed to use the World Wide Web.
- To introduce effective and efficient methods for searching for information on the Web.
- To create an interesting pre-conference/meeting activity.

Group Size

Any size. Subgroups can be formed and assigned different topics for research.

Time Required

Forty-five to fifty minutes.

Materials

- One copy of the Virtual Scavenger Hunt: Surfing the Web handout, sent to each participant prior to the event.
- One of the Virtual Scavenger Hunt lists for each participant, sent prior to the event.
- A computer linked with the World Wide Web for each participant or subgroup, if possible.
- A flip chart and felt-tipped markers for each subgroup.
- Token prizes, such as corporate logo items, if desired.

Physical Setting

A classroom, conference room, or seating area large enough for the group to work comfortably. Ideally each subgroup would have access to a computer linked with the World Wide Web, although it is not critical to the activity.

Process

1. Two to three weeks prior to the event, send each participant one copy of one of the Virtual Scavenger Hunt lists and one copy of the Virtual Scavenger Hunt: Surfing the Web handout. Inform participants that their completed Virtual Scavenger Hunt lists are their "tickets" for admission to the event. Give them the particulars about the event, such as place, date, and purpose.

2. When participants arrive, ask them to show you their completed lists. Give prizes to attendees who have completed their lists.

3. Pair those who finished with someone who did not. If the group is large or if you assigned different lists, seat participants by subgroup and give each subgroup a flip chart and markers. (*Note:* If you have fewer than twelve participants, subgroups are not necessary.)

4. Ask each subgroup to record on its flip chart the most interesting or original site address they found in answer to each question. (Ten to fifteen minutes.)

5. When the subgroups have written their master lists of site addresses, ask each group to share one or two that were particularly interesting with the large group. Assure them that you will collect the flip-chart sheets and send out a master list of all the sites that were discovered. (Ten minutes.)

6. If computers are available for each subgroup, allow them to search for several of the sites that were identified. If only one computer is available, ask participants to choose several sites. Then walk through the process of accessing them with the large group. (Ten minutes.)

7. Summarize the activity by asking the group the following questions:

   ■ How did you conduct the search?

   ■ What tools or techniques did you find useful?

   ■ How much time did it take you to complete your Virtual Scavenger Hunt? How long would it have taken to locate the same information by conventional, non-Web methods?

- What tips or techniques would you suggest to save time or increase the quality of Web searches in the future?
- What was your key learning from the Virtual Scavenger Hunt?

(Fifteen to twenty minutes.)

8. Collect the flip-chart sheets and completed Virtual Scavenger Hunt forms. Tell participants that you will distribute a summary of Web addresses to them and be sure to follow up to do so.

Variations

- A point-to-point scavenger hunt can be designed, in which the first question sends a participant to a specific site that contains a clue to the location of the next site, with final answers at the end of a trail from site to site.

- A scavenger hunt can be created to focus on the Web sites of a particular company or industry group, for competitor analysis or as part of new-employee orientation. Professional organizations or industry associations known to participants can be highlighted.

- The "hunt" can be timed in a virtual classroom or if enough computers are available on site. Release the scavenger hunt lists via e-mail and award a prize to the first person to respond with correct answers. (This will only work if all participants start at the same time.)

- The Virtual Scavenger Hunt can be used for a team event, particularly if the questions are very specific.

- Seasonal themes or traditional company events can provide a focus for the scavenger hunt.

Submitted by Jean G. Lamkin and Stanley L. Lamkin.

Jean G. Lamkin, Ph.D., is the corporate training director for Landmark Communications, Inc. She is also an adjunct professor at The George Washington University and president of the Park Institute, Ltd., a firm focused on assisting organizations in improving workforce performance. Her experience in training includes program and course design, evaluation, supervision, and leadership.

Stanley L. Lamkin, Ph.D., is a senior information technology manager for the Digital Equipment Corporation. He is also the principal Internet technology consultant for the Park Institute, Ltd. He has 20 years of computer research and management experience, including authoring 52 technical publications.

VIRTUAL SCAVENGER HUNT 1: MAKE MINE PASTA

Instructions: You have the opportunity of a lifetime to be served the world's finest Italian dinner. This is your chance to order exactly what you want. You make the decisions. But first you must shop around a bit and locate just the right ingredients, those that will satisfy your desires. Head for the nearest computer with Internet access and start searching. List the Internet address where you found your selections.

Your Shopping List	Internet Web Address
A bottle of Chianti or Pinot Grigio	_____
A source of fresh pasta	_____
Crusty Italian bread	_____
Checkered tablecloth and napkins	_____
Background music from a favorite opera	_____
A gourmet Italian cookbook	_____
Sauce, parmesan cheese, and sausage	_____
Long-burning candles	_____
Weather forecast	_____
Excellent cappuccino	_____
Your name:	_____
e-mail address:	_____

VIRTUAL SCAVENGER HUNT 2: VACATION TIME

Instructions: Lean back, close your eyes, and start to dream about your annual vacation. Where will you go this year? Make plans using the World Wide Web. How will you travel? What will you see and do? Make yourself comfortable at the computer and start surfing the Web.

You Need To Know	Internet Web Address
City, town, resort, or country to visit	_____
What you can see or do there	_____
What you'd like most to eat	_____
Where you could stand for the pictures you will take home	_____
Name of the ideal hotel	_____
Special local events scheduled	_____
When you will be there	_____
Recommended restaurant	_____
Map of the area	_____
Transportation you will use	_____
Source for tourist information	_____
The best time of year to go	_____
Your name:	_____
e-mail address:	_____

Virtual Scavenger Hunt 3: What's Your Industry I.Q.?

Instructions: The World Wide Web is a great place to take a tour. The price is right, you pick the time, and, unlike in your public library, you can eat, drink, and make as much noise as you like while you visit. Head for the nearest computer with a connection to the Internet and see where you can find what you're looking for.

What You're Looking for	Internet Web Address
Your company's Web site	_____
A competitor's site	_____
Professional organization you belong to (or wish to join)	_____
Address of an industry site	_____
Site for a professional journal or an industry magazine	_____
Where to find the stock market value of your company or one in which you invest	_____
Recent news article about your company	_____
Site you could use to provide information to potential employees on local housing and other costs	_____
Map of the area where your business is headquartered	_____
The Web address where you can find daily business information	_____
Your name:	_____
e-mail address:	_____

VIRTUAL SCAVENGER HUNT: SURFING THE WEB

The target audience for this article includes novice Internet users. Experienced Web users will find this material to be quite basic. Our discussion includes a how-to description of "surfing" the Web. But why learn? Let's start with a story. One of the authors never learned to type. He earned a doctorate in computer physics, has spent a long career using various types of keyboards, and has typed thousands of pieces of text, but has never established a systematic way of typing. He uses the "hunt-and-peck" method, which has adversely affected his efficiency.

Certain basic skills can be seen as key to our future success, simply by applying common sense. We *can* succeed by force of will if those skills are not acquired and we are willing to sacrifice efficiency; however, why travel that path?

The basic skill for "knowledge workers" in the 21st Century will be Web surfing. The quick acquisition of knowledge snippets will be the everyday lingua franca for value-added service providers. Those who employ the "hunt-and-peck" method for Web surfing will be doomed to inefficiency.

WHAT IS WEB SURFING?

The Web is both a physically connected (networked) set of worldwide computers and an extensive database organized somewhat like a library. Library materials are produced and housed by content providers within each computer linked to the Web. There is no central librarian, and content is not regulated. The only central authority is Network Solutions Corporation, which has exclusive rights to assign Internet protocol (IP) addresses for each Internet computer site (domain). So the Web is like a Library of Congress or ISBN system. Just as the Library of Congress does not regulate your book content, no one regulates what is on the Web.

The key difference between using a library system and using the Web is "hyperlinking." Hypertext Markup Language (HTML) is an electronic method of moving from one piece of subject matter to another using the Graphical User Interface (GUI) available on Microsoft Windows 3.1, Microsoft Windows 95, Microsoft NT, Apple Macintosh, and any UNIX system.

So What?

The Web contains very useful information within easy keystroke reach. For example, directions and the driving distances between cities are available from the Yahoo Web site at *http://www.yahoo.com*. Travel directions and maps for most addresses within the United States are easily found. Yahoo is only one of a dozen good sources of similar information.

- Want investment information? Visit the Lycos Web site at *http://www.lycos. com* and click on the investment subcategory under the Money category.

- Want quick access to an array of baseball material? Visit the Infoseek Web site at *http://infoseek.com*. Click on the baseball subcategory under the Sports category.

Yahoo, Lycos, and Infoseek are just three members of a large class of Web-based knowledge management tools call "search engines."

Access to the Internet

What does "visit a Web site" actually mean? First, establish a Web connection. You need a computer, of course, with either a company-provided network connection (generally a high speed intranet) or your own connection via an Internet service provider (ISP). To access an ISP such as AOL, MSN, Earthlink, Netcom, or Digex, you need a computer, modem, and telephone line. The ISP will provide Internet connection software and a connection (IP address) for you to access the Web. Typical monthly cost is $20 for unlimited access. Local ISPs tend to be less expensive, but deal with a national provider, such as the ones mentioned earlier, if you travel frequently. One nice aspect of the larger providers is that they use local telephone numbers. Local ISPs support very few local dialing exchanges and are expensive to use.

Two key decisions must be made: type of ISP and modem access speed.

ISP Type

Full-service providers, such as AOL and MSN, provide structured content as well as raw access to the Web, which works very well for rookie users.

Raw-access providers, such as Netcom and Earthlink, provide robust access to the Web and some value-added features, such as individualized home pages. However, their primary use is to provide unstructured access to the Web.

Modem Speed

Terms such as "throughput" and "bandwidth" are used to describe the rate at which digitized data is moved to and from a PC and the Internet server. Speed is important because graphics-intensive data requires high speeds to "download" data in a reasonable amount of time.

At the present time, the *minimum* acceptable speed is 14.4 kb/second modem. The current baseline is the 33.6 kb/sec used by U.S. Robotics, Zoom, and Gateway Telepath. The current high-speed modem (best for graphics) runs at 56 kb/sec, but the 56K standards have not been established as yet. First, ask your ISP which ones are supported. 56K is nice, and modems (for example, Zoom) can be obtained for about $100.

For high-speed access (128 kb/sec), employ an ISDN connection. Just call the local telephone company for details. These systems will cost $50–$90/ month, depending on geographic location. ISDN lines are finicky and require patience and a certain level of user sophistication.

An important, but not key, decision involves choice of a "browser," which enables the Web-based page and takes care of the details of electronically displaying the data for you. There are two primary choices:

- *Internet Explorer.* From Microsoft *(http://www.microsoft.com)*. This is a free browser and can be seamlessly integrated into your desktop. Version 4.0 is available as a free download.

- *Netscape Navigator* or *Communicator.* From Netscape *(http://home.netscape. com)*. This is also a free browser. Available in version 4.0, this browser was once head-and-shoulders above all others. It still edges Internet Explorer (in our opinion), but the two are very close.

The bottom line is that you cannot go wrong with either choice.

Search Engines

Let's say that you are in a large public library and are trying to locate specific information on growing potatoes. You can locate the library catalog and look for information under potatoes, gardening, agriculture, horticulture, botany, vegetables, and so on. You could also consult a subject-matter expert, who could recommend books or trade publications.

Web surfing uses "search engines" in a similar way. Search engines are freely provided computer programs that locate and report Web sites that contain information related to your specified search criteria. The search engines also provide a way to hyperlink to the referenced sites. They include both unstructured and structured searches.

Unstructured search engines use "Web crawling" software that laboriously goes to every worldwide Internet site, categorizes the key words (keyword in computer jargon) in each piece of informational text, and records them in a database repository. To search you would look for key words, such as potato, gardening, or botany, and the database would respond with associated sites. You then would visit each site as you would a library book to determine which suit your needs. These are generally referred to as "ad hoc" search queries, because they provide a nonprioritized list of all locations containing the key words.

The structured site both crawls the Web and pre-categorizes information. It will give a selection of sites pertaining to a desired topic area. All three of the sites mentioned above (Yahoo, Lycos, and Infoseek) are structured sites that allow for unstructured Web searches as well.

A good site to find search engine links in one place is the Netscape home page. Click on the Netscape icon on your desktop (after installation). When the home page loads, click once on the "N" icon in the upper right-hand corner. This will take you to Netscape's home page. Then click on the tool bar icon called Internet search. This will take you to a site containing many search engines. Most search engines in use today will allow both types of searches, but not in equal proportions.

The best-known structured search engine is Yahoo *(http://www.yahoo. com)*. Yahoo, like Infoseek, Lycos, and Excite, has pre-searched the Web, edited the data, and assigned the information into subject areas. This approach seeks to minimize the number of "garbage" sites that inevitably appear during an unstructured search, but each categorization strategy is different. Let's say you are interested in cars. Infoseek displays a category called "Buy a car." No such category exists for Yahoo, but if you type "automobile" into the search box for Yahoo, it leads to some indexed categories related to cars. Certain types of information are more readily obtained from one structured search engine than from others. The differences must be learned through experience.

A good example of an unstructured search engine is Altavista *(http:// altavista.digital.com)*, which features a comprehensive database of Web content and a very rapid key word search algorithm. Typing the key word "automobile" into the search window provides more than a million entries—far too many to examine in a single lifetime. A major entry is the Japan Automotive Society *(http://japan.auto.com)*. Unstructured searches are beneficial for purposes of serendipity. They are also good for searches that contain highly specific key words. Altavista, which is probably the best search engine for the intermediate-to-advanced user, contains a structured set of categories that provide guidance, but do not take control in the way that Yahoo-type engines do. As a point of interest, Altavista provides a free piece of software, called "personal extensions," that will search and index your hard disk. This allows you to search through your own information using key words. This feature is very handy for professionals.

Push Technology

As discussed, the Web contains a massive amount of easily accessed information. Free "download" products such as Pointcast from *http://www.pointcast.com* provide the next generation of knowledge tools, called "Push Technology." The concept is simple. Consider Cable TV. There are news channels like CNN, arts networks like A&E and BRAVO, and special-interest channels like the Black Entertainment Network (BET). These channels "push" specific information based on individual preferences. Web products, such as Pointcast, ask for your topical interest areas and then decide what information to "push" onto your browser. The interfaces are well designed and convey a sense of up-to-date topical relevance.

Pointcast also includes numerous special-interest categories, including government, banking, automotive, aerospace, and computers. Pointcast updates information (weather, news, industry) several times a day and transmits it to your browser. This can be used as a screen saver also.

SUMMARY

The Web contains the world's largest free public lending library. The library includes a set of categories similar to a library's card catalog to locate information and a set of "push" channels similar to cable TV. The challenge for the knowledge worker of the 21st Century will be to gain a level of familiarity and comfort with the disparate search tools available on the Web. The key is to obtain sufficient experience with the tools to determine which set can support your goals most effectively.

620. The Affinity Diagram: Introducing a Tool

Goals

- To introduce the concept of an affinity diagram.
- To demonstrate the use of the affinity diagram.

Group Size

Ten to thirty participants.

Time Required

Twenty to thirty minutes.

Materials

- A gummed name tag for each participant.
- A felt-tipped pen for each participant.

Physical Setting

A room with enough space for the group members to move around during the activity.

Process

1. Introduce the activity as a creative way to demonstrate how the affinity diagram works. Give one name tag and a felt-tipped pen to each participant and ask each to privately write the name of a famous person—alive or dead, real or fictional—on the name tag. (Five minutes.)

2. After they have all written names, ask them to place their name tags on the *backs* of the individuals sitting to their right. (If the participants are sitting in any type of configuration other than circular, someone will have to walk the end person's name tag over to the "first" person.)

3. Ask the participants if they remember the game "Twenty Questions." Say that the next step is like "Twenty Questions" in that they can ask only closed-ended questions of one another until they guess the names written on the name tags on their backs. Ask the participants to stand. Encourage them to mingle and to ask different people different questions. Tell them that when they have guessed their names, they can move their name tags from their backs to the fronts of their clothing. (Five minutes.)

4. After five minutes, if you still have some participants with name tags on their backs, tell the other participants to offer those persons "clues." Within two minutes, all participants should have moved their name tags to their fronts. (Two minutes.)

5. Call time and reconvene the group. Explain to the participants that they now have a list of famous people and that such a list is often generated by brainstorming. Say that the next step is to do a "silent sort," which is the real power of the affinity diagram. Explain that, during the silent sort, each of them is to silently move and stand next to a "famous person" with whom his or her own famous person has an "affinity" or something in common. Explain that once they move, they are not to look around to see if there are better "fits." Tell them that it is okay to make "clusters" of famous people and that, if they do not have anything in common with others, it is okay to stand alone. Tell them that you will give a fifteen-second countdown when it appears to you that they are close to being finished. Say that when the countdown is over, they should stop moving.

6. Allow the participants to sort themselves in silence (you may have to reinforce the silence with a few "shhhhhs") for three or four minutes. Then start counting down from fifteen to zero aloud. When you reach zero, remind them that they must stop moving. (Five minutes.)

7. Move to each cluster (or individual standing alone) and ask for a word, phrase, or statement that captures the flavor or essence of the famous people represented. (Five minutes.)

8. Reconvene the group and say that this process models the affinity diagram tool. First, a list is generated by brainstorming, research, or some other method. Then the items on the list are sorted, for example, by customer type. The result is an "affinity diagram," similar to the participants' physical clustering.

9. Guide a discussion of the activity. The following questions may be helpful:

   ■ What happened during the process?

- What do you see as the greatest benefit of using the affinity diagram process?

- How could you use the affinity diagram tool on the job?

(Five minutes.)

10. Conclude by stating that the affinity diagram is a tool that they can use when they have a large number of items that must be sorted quickly.

Variations

- If pressed for time, omit the "Twenty Questions" part and just ask the participants to place their name tags on the fronts of their clothing.

- This activity works well as an energizer if the group members already are familiar with the affinity diagram.

Submitted by Kristin Arnold.

Kristin Arnold maintains a private consulting practice. She specializes in facilitation services and training, with an emphasis on strategic planning, strategic partnerships, collaborative problem solving, and team building. Ms. Arnold has extensive experience as both an internal and external consultant with a wide variety of manufacturing and service industries, as well as the government sector.

621. Take Note of Yourself: A Team-Development Activity

Goals

- To become better acquainted with individuals in a group or team.
- To identify and discuss differences among members of a team.
- To have an opportunity to discuss how differences may affect the team in the future.

Group Size

Eight to twenty members of a team who are not yet well acquainted.

Time Required

Forty to fifty minutes.

Materials

- Post-it® Notes, at least six per participant.
- A pen, pencil, or marker for each participant.
- A flip chart and felt-tipped markers for the facilitator.

Physical Setting

A room that is large enough for participants to move around and plenty of wall space for posting Post-it® Notes.

Process

1. Distribute six Post-it® Notes to each participant. Ask the participants to write adjectives or phrases that describe one of their physical features,

interests, characteristics, or attitudes on five of the notes, one descriptive word or phrase per note. Participants should sign their initials on each note. (Five minutes.)

2. Ask the participants to write a quality or feature that is *not commonly known* about them on the sixth note. Participants should *not* add their initials to this note. (One minute.)

3. When the participants have finished, ask them to post their notes on the wall. Designate a specific place for the notes with no initials, separate from the notes with initials.

4. After all notes have been posted, have the participants walk around, read one another's notes, and then select several initialed notes that interest them. Tell them to take the notes, approach other participants at random, and ask if each note could apply to them or is actually the person's note. If they find the individual who wrote a note, they are to ask the person to explain why he or she selected this particular adjective or phrase to describe himself or herself. If the person approached did not write that particular note, participants are to inquire whether the phrase is like or unlike the person and why. Each participant should speak with at least three others. (Fifteen to twenty minutes.)

5. Monitor the activity to observe the level and type of interactions. Ask everyone to be seated.

6. To summarize the activity, ask the following questions, posting answers on the flip chart:

   ▪ What criteria did you use to select the notes you did?

   ▪ Why did you approach the individuals you did?

   ▪ How comfortable were you when approaching people you did not know well or discussing notes you were interested in?

   ▪ What differences did you discover among individuals?

   ▪ How might those differences influence how you work together as a team?

   (Fifteen to twenty minutes.)

7. Ask one or two individuals to collect and read the unsigned notes aloud. Ask the participants what each statement might mean and what implications it may have for the person when working with a group. (Fifteen minutes.)

8. Conclude the activity by summarizing some of the statements from the flip chart. State that the future success of any team will be, to some extent, dependent on knowing the strengths and preferences of each team member. Encourage participants to continue to learn more about individuals on their team and to consider what they have learned when working with any team in the future.

Variations

- After everyone has met several new people, form subgroups. Post the questions from Step 6 and have the subgroups explore the questions before reconvening the larger group.
- Form subgroups to identify the authors of the unsigned notes. Award a token prize for the subgroup with the highest number of correct matches.
- Have the group select distinctive notes based on criteria such as most unusual, humorous, or intriguing description.

Submitted by Michael P. Bochenek.

Michael P. Bochenek, Ph.D., is an assistant professor of business administration at Elmhurst College in Elmhurst, Illinois. He teaches human resource management, organization behavior, negotiation, management, and compensation courses. He has twenty-five years of human resource experience with a telecommunications firm. His research interests include innovative management practices and paradoxes. His work has been published in the 1998 Annual *and the* Management Development Forum. *He received his Ph.D. in sociology from Loyola University in Chicago.*

622. Jigsaw Puzzles: Providing Resources and Feedback

Goals

- To demonstrate the value of providing resources and feedback while a group is completing a task.

- To identify criteria necessary to complete tasks more effectively.

Group Size

As many as twenty-five participants, divided into at least three subgroups of four to six people each.

Time Required

Forty-five minutes to one hour.

Materials

- Sixty-piece jigsaw puzzles, a different one for each subgroup, in separate plastic self-sealing bags.
- Blank paper and pens or pencils for the expert/observers.
- A flip chart and felt-tipped markers for the facilitator.
- Masking tape.

Physical Setting

A room large enough for the subgroups to work without distracting one another and a table for each subgroup.

Process

1. Set the stage by asking the participants, "What problems do people in your organization or work area encounter when they are given new tasks?" Record their comments on the flip chart. (Five minutes.)

2. Say that the problems they have listed are probably not uncommon in most organizations. Say that certain practices help to eliminate some of these problems and increase the effectiveness of task accomplishment. Add that the activity they are about to participate in will help to demonstrate this point.

3. Ask the participants to raise their hands if they rate their own jigsaw-puzzle assembly skills and/or understanding of the process at a seven or higher on a ten-point scale. Designate these people as the "expert/observers," who will be used as the activity progresses to help non-experts to understand the process. Tell them that they will begin as observers and end as advisors. Give each expert/observer blank paper and a pen or pencil. (Five minutes.)

4. Organize the group into subgroups of four to six members each, ensuring that at least half the members of each group consider themselves to be non-experts.

5. Tell the non-experts that they will assemble the puzzles. Tell the expert/observers that they are to remain silent, as passive observers, until they are instructed differently.

6. Distribute the plastic bags containing the puzzle pieces—without providing the matching puzzle boxes, one bag to each subgroup.

7. Explain that there will be three, five-minute rounds of puzzle assembly. Each round will be followed by one minute of feedback to improve task accomplishment. Say that you will act as timekeeper and will provide instructions before and after each round.

8. Inform the participants that, in Round 1, only the assemblers may talk to one another. The expert/observers must observe silently. They may not point to or touch any of the puzzle pieces, and they must record their observations silently. Begin Round 1. (Five minutes.)

9. Call time and announce that the members of each subgroup have a few minutes to give one another feedback on how to improve their performance. (Two minutes.)

10. Ask each subgroup to share the suggestions its members exchanged. Record the suggestions on the flip chart as "peer feedback." (Ten minutes.)

11. Ask the subgroups to take their puzzles apart and to place the pieces back in their bags. Then ask the subgroups to move clockwise to different work tables, leaving the puzzles they worked on behind.

12. Before Round 2, state that the assemblers and the expert/observers may talk with one another during this round. Expert/observers may provide oral feedback, but may not point to or touch puzzle pieces. Begin the round. (Five minutes.)

13. After Round 2, ask if the feedback time at the end of the last round was helpful. After soliciting a few responses, allow one or two minutes for the subgroup members to give one another feedback about how they could improve. When they have finished, ask each subgroup to share the suggestions its members exchanged. Again, record the suggestions on the flip chart as "peer feedback." (Ten minutes.)

14. Ask the subgroups to take their puzzles apart, place them in the bags, and move on to new tables.

15. Before Round 3, state that assemblers and expert/observers may also talk during this round and that the expert/observers may point to and touch puzzle pieces this time. However, the job of assembling the pieces still belongs to the assemblers. Finally, give each group the box showing its puzzle picture and begin the round. (Six minutes.)

16. After Round 3, reconvene the total group and facilitate a brief discussion, using the following questions:

■ How was each round different for you?

■ Compare the experience of assembling the puzzle in Round 1, with no feedback from the expert/observers, with your experience in Round 2.

■ Compare the experience of assembling the puzzle in Round 2, with feedback but without the picture, to the experience of assembling the puzzle with the aid of the picture and feedback in Round 3.

■ What difference did exchanging feedback after each round make?

■ What difference did talking to the expert/observers, receiving feedback, and having the picture make?

■ Sometimes your work tasks may feel as though someone dumped puzzle pieces in your lap without providing the picture. What are you doing, or can you do, in your organization to obtain the overall picture and find out how the pieces fit?

- What are some examples of the "big picture" in your organization?

- Can you see various levels of the "big picture" within your organization (e.g., what customers expect, the organizational mission, reasons for tasks)? What are the levels in your organization?

(Fifteen to twenty minutes.)

Variations

- This activity can be used for team building.

- The activity can be used for communication training, with the following changes: In Round 1, everyone is silent, both assemblers and expert/observers; in Round 2, assemblers may talk, but expert/observers must be silent; and in Round 3, everyone may talk.

- The activity can be used in supervisory/management training to illustrate the importance of effective task instructions and feedback. In this situation, use the following questions to debrief the activity:

  - What types of feedback were useful and what types were not useful?

  - What were the differences between Round 1, in which the expert/observers were instructed to be silent, and the rounds in which they gave their suggestions?

  - How did the expert/observers' actions in Rounds 2 and 3 affect the completion of the puzzle? Were they helpful or did they get in the way?

Submitted by Brian Korzec and Mary Anne Newkirk.

Brian Korzec, M.S., is founder and director of the Center for Personal and Organizational Change. He has served as a process consultant, facilitator, and educator with individuals, groups, national and international organizations, and nonprofit and government agencies. Since 1996, he has dedicated himself to working as an internal organization development consultant with the federal government's Health Care Finance Administration (HCFA) to build an effective learning community.

Mary Anne Newkirk, M.S., *is the owner of CHANGEWORKS, a training and consulting company that helps individuals and organizations to build the resilience to thrive in today's business environment. Her specialties include change management, teams, group facilitation, and the personal-mastery skills of conflict management and time management. She received her master's degree in applied behavioral science from Johns Hopkins University. She currently serves on the board of the Chesapeake Bay Organization Development Network.*

623. Koosh® Ball Company: Experiencing the Difference Between Process Improvement and Reengineering

Goals

- To demonstrate the difference between continuous process improvement and reengineering a process.

- To demonstrate the need for innovation when reengineering a process.

- To develop participants' awareness of behaviors that may obstruct or undermine innovation.

- To develop participants' awareness of behaviors that may contribute to process innovation.

Group Size

Ten to twenty participants.

Time Required

Fifty-five to sixty minutes.

Materials

- A set of three Koosh® balls or any soft balls (palm size) in three different colors.

- A stop watch.

- A prepared overhead transparency or flip-chart sheet of the Koosh® Ball Company Policy and appropriate markers.

- Paper and a pencil or pen for recording data.

Physical Setting

A room large enough for the team to toss balls around. A hallway can be used if necessary.

Process

1. Explain to the group that they are workers for the Koosh® Ball Company. Take out the three balls of different colors.

2. Say to the group, "I have three balls of x color, y color, and z color. I am going to toss each ball to one person in order, x, y, z. After you catch the balls, select someone else in the room and toss all three balls to that person, in the same order. That person will do the same until everyone in the room has had a chance to catch all three balls." Repeat the instructions if necessary, but do not go into further detail.

3. Toss the three balls to one person. Record this person's name on a sheet of paper for future reference. As the balls are tossed between participants, make no comment, and express no indication of whether they are correct or not.

4. When the last person has caught all three balls, ask if there is anyone who did not catch all three balls. If someone has not, continue until the last person has all three balls. Collect the three balls from the last person and record this person's name. (Five minutes.)

5. Announce to the group:

   "I am the president of the Koosh® Ball Company and am quite disappointed in your performance. During this process, balls were damaged (dropped) and passed incorrectly [wrong order of balls, same person receiving them more than once, etc.] and it took a long time for the process. Accordingly, I have decided to develop a simple process which, if followed correctly, should improve your efficiency, eliminate damage, and reduce repetition."

6. Display the Koosh® Ball Company Policy overhead or flip-chart sheet. Read it to the group. Do not solicit questions. If any are asked at any point, refer the person to the policy.

7. Give the three balls to the same person who started the last time. Tell the person to begin, by shouting "Start." When the last person (the same as the original process) catches all three balls, he or she is to shout "Stop." Advise participants that you will time the process this time.

8. When the first person shouts "Start," start the stop watch. Also record observations about the process as balls are passed between participants. When the last person shouts "Stop," stop the stop watch. Record the time in a corner of the Koosh® Ball Company Policy display so that everyone can see it.

9. Tell participants that while they were busy with this process an opportunity was presented to you from a company in Singapore. Tell participants:

"My sources in Singapore claim that if I close down this plant and move all production to Singapore, the workers there can not only eliminate damage and waste (repetition), but can improve on your processing time. Now, I like all of you, and would rather not close down this plant, but it is an attractive offer. My challenge to you is to eliminate damage and waste and improve on your processing time. Then perhaps I'll consider keeping the operation here going."

10. Give the three balls to the same person who started the last time. Tell him or her that when everyone is ready to shout "Start," and remind the group that the last person should shout "Stop" after catching the last three balls. Say that you will again time the process.

11. When the first person shouts "Start," start the stop watch, record your observations about the process, and stop timing when the last person shouts "Stop." Record the time next to the first time and mark it as number two.

12. After this round, tell the group:

"While you were working on the process, I had an opportunity presented to me from a company in Mexico. They claim that if I close down my plant and move the production to Mexico, they cannot only eliminate damage and waste (repetition), but can improve on the processing time. I am impressed by the improved time during this last round, as well as the decrease in waste and damage. I would rather not close down this plant, but it is an attractive offer. My challenge to you is to ensure that there is no damage or waste and to improve on the processing time. Then perhaps I'll consider keeping the operation here."

13. Give the three balls to the same person who started the last process. Tell the person that when he or she is ready to shout "Start." When the last person (as per the original process) catches all three balls, he or she is to shout "Stop." Advise participants that you will time the process.

14. Follow the same process, marking the time as number three.

15. Again, address all of the participants. Tell them:

> "While this process was going on, I had an opportunity to talk to a number of consultants who have worked with similar processes in other organizations. They claim that this process can be done in less than one second. I said, 'No way.' They said they could show us how, but can not come for another week. They suggested firing all of you and replacing you with new employees who have fresh ideas. Now, as I said before, I really do like all of you and would rather not fire you, but it is an attractive idea to be able to process the Koosh® balls in less than one second. I could make a lot more money. My challenge to you is to reduce the processing time to one second or less on the next round or I'll have to fire all of you."

16. Give the three balls to the same person who started the last process. Tell the participants that you need to leave for a few minutes and that you suggest that the team take some time to discuss the challenge ahead of them. Tell them to call you when they are ready for you to time the process again. Move away from the group and allow them time to identify a radically new approach. (Ten to fifteen minutes.)

17. When they call you back, time the process one last time and record it again. Applaud their efforts. (*Note:* The group may come up with a solution sooner. If so, you will of course shorten the activity.) Two of the possible solutions are listed at the end of the activity.

18. Bring closure with the following questions:

- What happened to people's innovative ideas early in the process?
- Why can innovative ideas be blocked in the day-to-day work environment? How does that happen?
- What managerial behaviors encourage innovative ideas? Discourage them?
- At the beginning of the process, you were looking for ways to *continuously improve* the process. Then the climate changed, and you had to *reengineer* the process. What are the differences between the two?
- What role does innovation play in reengineering?
- Why didn't the team immediately decide to strive for a one-second process?

(Twenty minutes.)

19. Review the notes you took during each process with the group. You may wish to read your notes about what was said (not who said it) and how others reacted. Undoubtedly, the comments would be things like "Can't do that," "That's not in the rules," or "It's against our policy."

Variation

- With groups larger than twenty, divide participants into teams of ten to twenty and assign an observer to each team.

Potential Solutions

There are many solutions. Two of them follow:

- Each person creates a funnel with his or her hands by placing the thumbs and fingertips of both hands together to form a circular shape. Then each person places his or her hands on top of another's in the original order to form a funnel from top to bottom. Some people may have to crouch, while other stretch above them. The starting person drops all three balls in the order of x, y, z colors so that each ball passes through the people's hands to the last person.

- All the team members stand together to form a tight circle around the first person, facing in. They hold up the palms of their hands in front of them, facing the center person. The first person holds the three balls in the correct order and spins around, touching each person's hands in the order of x, y, z colors.

Submitted by Michael Stanleigh.

Michael Stanleigh, president of Business Improvement Architects, is a management consultant and award-winning trainer who specializes in strategic planning, executive coaching, project management, leadership, reengineering, and process analysis. He has spoken at many conferences and has written articles that have been published in many countries on the subjects of innovation, total quality, employee motivation, management, and human resource development. He teaches Developing and Leading Effective Engineering Project Teams at the University of Toronto in Ontario, Canada.

Koosh® Ball Company Policy

- Balls must be passed in the same order:

  - X color

  - Y color

  - Z color

- Balls must be passed in the same order from person to person

- Everyone must touch the balls

624. Openers: Making Connections

Goal

- To provide a structure for participants to meet others in large groups or crowds.

Group Size

Any number.

Time Required

Thirty minutes.

Materials

- A microphone for the facilitator.
- Soft balls or wads of paper for groups.

Physical Setting

Any room in which a large group has gathered, ideally with plenty of space for moving about.

Process

1. Welcome the participants, using the microphone if necessary. Introduce the activity by stating that the goal is for everyone in the group to meet as many others as possible in a short time period.

2. Lead the participants through as many of the following activities as possible in fifteen or twenty minutes.

   - Stand up and shake hands with everyone around you.
   - Stand up and shift to the right or left, shake hands, and introduce yourself to one new person.

- Form groups of four or five. Remain standing and take one minute to share two pieces of personal information from the following list:
    - Home town
    - Nickname
    - Hobby
    - One creative thing you have done
    - One creative thing you would like to do
    - One strange gift you have received or given
- Form groups by state or region and introduce yourselves.
- Create a "wave," like a stadium wave.
- Find someone who lives in a city that starts with the same letter as your city.
- Form circles of four to five. Using old tennis balls, foam balls, or wadded paper, throw an object around the circle in alphabetical order by first name.
- Form groups of eight to ten and throw the same object in alphabetical order.
- Throw the object in reverse alphabetical order.
- Place yourself in a line in alphabetical order *non-verbally*. (In a large auditorium, people can stay in their rows.)
- Have the entire group line up in alphabetical order.
- Form a line by years with the organization or by any other criteria.

3. Tell the group when there are two minutes left. You may wish to ask if they would like to continue for a few extra minutes. Then ask everyone to return to their original seats.

4. Ask for a show of hands for how many people met more than five people or ten people or twenty people.

5. Suggest that they follow up with their new acquaintances at the next break.

Variation

- Develop a specific list of activities based on the topic, location, organization, or time of year.

Submitted by Robert Alan Black.

***Robert Alan Black, Ph.D.**, is an independent consultant and professional speaker who specializes in speaking, training, and facilitation, with an emphasis on the enhancement and application of creative thinking in the workplace through development of skills in coordinating, communicating, collaborating, and creating. Dr. Black has extensive experience with business, industry, educational, and government sector clients.*

625. Your Voice, Your Self: Improving Vocal Presentations

Goals

- To provide feedback for speakers in a small group.
- To illustrate the importance of voice quality when giving presentations.

Group Size

Ten to twelve people interested in improving their vocal presentation styles.

Time Required

One hour to an hour and twenty minutes.

Materials

- One copy of the Your Voice, Your Self Vocal Presentations Style Sheet for each participant.
- Multiple copies of the Vocal Presentations Style Checklist for each participant. Participants will complete one for each of the other participants; if there are ten participants, you will need 90.
- A large decorative shopping bag to hold twenty speech starters.
- Twenty speech starters: An assortment of common objects found in the home or work settings, such as a candle, book of matches, small date book, large paper clip, glue stick, feather, stick-on notes, pen, screwdriver, compass, paint brush, crayons, dime, or ball. (Location-specific items can also be included, such as a football game program, movie schedule, rock, shell, souvenir, or anything small enough for the bag.)

Physical Setting

Tables and chairs in a U-shaped formation.

Process

1. Deliver a lecturette on vocal presentation style based on the Your Voice, Your Self Vocal Presentations Style Sheet. When you have finished, provide participants with copies of the handout for future reference. Also give everyone enough copies of the Your Voice, Your Self Vocal Presentations Style Checklists to evaluate everyone else in the group. (Five minutes.)

2. Review the terms "voice rate," "volume," "pitch," "inflection," and "articulation" by asking participants to explain the terms in their own words. (Five minutes.)

3. Ask each participant to draw one item from the bag. Give them a few minutes to compose short speeches telling others how the item relates to them. Explain that the speech can be about the past, about a present characteristic or event, or about a future goal or event. (For example, stick-on notes might prompt a talk about a person's organizational methods or the lack thereof or a candle may prompt a memory of a mother's collection of candles or a time the lights went out.) Tell participants to make their presentations about one minute in length. Answer any questions participants may have. (Five minutes.)

4. Have participants take turns giving their speeches while other members of the group complete their assessments and pass the sheets to you. Be sure to allow enough time for people to fill in comments, if desired.

5. After all participants have spoken, return the checklists to the appropriate individuals. Ask each person to read the feedback received and to write a brief summary of his or her own vocal presentation style on the back of the sheet, based on the comments received. Ask them to identify two things they did well and two things they wish to improve. (Ten minutes.)

6. Debrief by asking people to respond to the following:

   ■ What are some of the things you did well?

   ■ In what ways can you improve your oral presentations in the future?

   ■ What was not difficult for you about this activity?

   ■ How can you improve your voice rate, pitch, inflection, or articulation?

   (Ten minutes.)

Variations

- A video camera can be used, with individual tapes of each person, if possible, so that they can review the tapes prior to writing their summaries.

- The items in the shopping bag can be selected specifically for the participant group.

Submitted by Taggart Smith.

Taggart Smith, Ed.D., is an associate professor in the Department of Organizational Leadership and Supervision, School of Technology, Purdue University, West Lafayette, Indiana. His areas of expertise include conference leadership and developing managers of training in organizations. He is a member of the Association of Business Communication and the American Society for Engineering Education, where he is chair of the Engineering Management Division.

YOUR VOICE, YOUR SELF VOCAL PRESENTATIONS STYLE SHEET

The purpose of communication is to transfer information and how you feel about this information to others. Whether you are enthusiastic about sharing information is shown by your body language or nonverbal communication, which includes posture, gestures, facial expressions, eye contact, and "presence." Indeed, it is generally known that visual clues (what is seen) form over half of the impact people have in face-to-face communication. In addition, vocal signals (sounds and tone of voice) create slightly less than half of the impact in communication. Strangely enough, the words themselves account for less than 10 percent of the impact. In other words, *how you deliver your message weighs more heavily in others' perceptions than the words you speak.*

Receiving feedback from others can be very beneficial as you seek to improve your communication style. You may not always agree with others' assessments (it is difficult to see ourselves as others see us), but they will give you a starting point for addressing your weaknesses and enhancing your strengths as a speaker.

Effective vocal delivery involves five factors: voice rate, volume, pitch, inflection, and articulation.

Voice Rate

Your voice rate depends on several of your characteristics—personality, cultural upbringing, degree of preparation for speaking, or locale. Rapid speech is fine, so long as you speak distinctly and bring your audience with you through your words. Speaking very slowly may cause listeners to tune you out. Strike a happy medium while maintaining your own style, as anything else may appear false.

One human tendency to avoid is filling in pauses in speaking with "uhms" and "uhs." Most of us are wary of silence or pauses, so when we're thinking of what to say next, we say "uh." Don't be afraid of silence; use pauses for emphasis.

Volume

The loudness or softness of your voice should depend on the size of your audience and the acoustics of the room you are in. Support your voice box by breathing with your diaphragm so that you can be heard by the audience. Speaking too loudly occurs less frequently in small groups, but it can happen. Remember to vary your volume, depending on the content of your message. Here's where you can really reach out to your audience!

Pitch

How high or low your voice goes is its pitch. You probably are aware of your pitch level in different situations—cheering the team at a ball game, conversing with someone at a party, reading to small children at bedtime. The best thing to do in a speech is to vary your pitch. Say some sentences in the higher ranges and some in the lower, just to make your voice more expressive. Try not to speak in a monotone (one or two pitches only). People listen more to an expressive voice.

Inflection

Which words you emphasize, the way you end sentences (rising tone or falling tone), your physical responsiveness to words—all make up inflection. Inflection sometimes is influenced by the culture in which you were raised, as well as the locale and the language you speak. Inflection is important in your delivery because it determines whether people will continue to listen once you have their attention. It is how your voice sounds to others.

Articulation

Articulation is dependant on whether you pronounce the endings of your words, the degree of distinctness with which you say words, and whether people can easily understand you. For better articulation, use your lips, open your mouth, and use your whole speaking mechanism to be better understood.

Remember that the key to a good presentation style begins with knowing how you come across to others.

YOUR VOICE, YOUR SELF VOCAL PRESENTATIONS STYLE CHECKLIST

Speaker's Name: _____

Rate

1. Could be slower _____ Could be faster _____ Good rate _____
2. Needs smoothing; choppy phrasing _____
   Phrasing OK; work on variety _____

Volume

1. Too soft _____ Too loud _____ Volume fine _____
2. Same volume throughout _____ Good variety _____

Pitch

1. Level could be lower _____ Level could be higher _____
   Level OK _____
2. Repetitive pitch pattern _____ Good variety _____

Inflection

1. Harsh sound _____ Timid sound _____ Tone OK _____
2. Flat sound _____ Rich, resonant sound _____

Articulation

1. Emphasize consonants more _____ Good, distinct words _____
2. Word endings omitted _____ Clear word delivery _____
3. Lips hardly moved _____ Good lip movement _____

Comments for the Speaker:

_____

_____

_____

_____

_____

_____

626. Building Blocks: Giving Clear Instructions

Goals

- To identify criteria necessary to write clear, accurate instructions.
- To experience what it is like to attempt a task with unclear written instructions.

Group Size

Eight to twenty-four participants in subgroups of four.

Time Required

One hour and fifteen minutes to two hours.

Materials

- One LEGO® System package for each subgroup. (These are individually packaged sets of small LEGO® blocks. Each package contains pieces to build a specific object, such as a car, tractor, or boat.)
- A supply of paper and pencils for each participant.
- A flip chart and markers for each subgroup.

Physical Setting

A large room for subgroup work and a separate breakout room for trainees to work.

Process

1. Introduce the activity by discussing the problems associated with learning to perform a new task by using written instructions. Ask participants to

describe some problems they have faced and list them on the flip chart by category, such as "jargon," "unclear," or "confusing." (Ten minutes.)

2. Explain that writing clear instructions requires breaking a task down into "steps" or sequential actions. Illustrate the use of steps with a common example, such as making toast or pumping gas. Have the large group list the steps and key ideas required and post them on a flip chart.

3. Discuss why it is important to include key ideas or why the steps must be performed in a specific way. Solicit ideas from the group. In addition, stress the importance of avoiding assumptions about a trainee's prior knowledge.

4. After listing everyone's comments on the flip chart, have participants form subgroups of four. Ensure that each subgroup has a flip chart, markers, paper, pencils, and a LEGO® System. Tell subgroups to appoint a recorder and a "new trainee."

5. Explain that the new trainees will leave the room while the other three members of each subgroup write training instructions for assembling the LEGO® System. The new trainees will then return and be asked to assemble the object according to the subgroups' written instructions.

6. Have the new trainees separate from the subgroups. Tell the remaining members in the subgroups to write instructions for assembling the toys. Let each group decide how to proceed. Answer any questions and let them begin.

7. Walk around the room, telling groups to have their recorders write their instructions on the flip charts when they are finished and to position their flip charts so that other groups will not see their instructions. (Twenty to twenty-five minutes.)

8. Assemble the new trainees in the breakout room. Give them paper and pencils and a flip chart with markers. Tell them to identify criteria they will use to judge the quality of the instructions and to list them on the flip chart. (For example, they may expect the instructions to use commonly defined words or to be in sequential order. Obviously, they should be able to assemble the toy!)

9. When all groups are ready, have the new trainees rejoin their respective subgroups and attempt to assemble the object by following the instructions on the flip chart. (Generally, the trainees will experience some confusion and the subgroups will have to explain one or more of the steps.) (Fifteen minutes.)

10. When all new trainees have finished, have each subgroup in turn display its fully assembled objects and flip-chart directions to the total group. Ask each trainee to share his or her experience. List comments on a flip chart. (Ten minutes.)

11. Have a representative of the trainee subgroup share its list of criteria for judging instructions with the large group. (Ten minutes.)

12. Have the subgroups re-form and compare their flip-chart instructions with their criteria. Ask them to prepare to report the differences to the large group. (Five minutes.)

13. Bring the large group together and review the learning from the activity by asking the following questions:

   ■ What are some characteristics of "good" instructions?

   ■ How did your subgroup's instructions compare with the criteria?

   ■ What are the advantages of breaking a task into steps or categories?

   ■ What did you learn about making assumptions?

   ■ How can what you have learned be applied to training others back on the job?

   (Fifteen to twenty minutes.)

Variations

■ Other sets of play building sets could be used, or participants could build paper airplanes or other paper objects.

■ Oral directions could be used instead of written directions.

■ Participants from an intact group could use a task that is done as part of their job, then share their analysis with a co-worker or supervisor.

■ Participants could be assigned to evaluate a training manual or other written instructions currently being used in their organization.

Submitted by Julie Furst-Bowe.

Julie Furst-Bowe, Ed.D., is an associate professor and program director for the graduate program in training and development at the University of Wisconsin-Stout. She teaches courses in training systems, instructional design, and multimedia applications. She is also the author of several articles on the use of instructional technology in training.

627. Tool Box: Reinforcing Concepts

Goal

- To review concepts and skills that were introduced in a training session.

Group Size

Eight to twenty participants.

Time Required

Twenty to thirty minutes.

Materials

- A set of 3" x 5" index cards with one phrase per card, identifying key concepts and skills that will be taught during the training session.
- Masking tape.
- A sheet of flip-chart paper posted on the wall or easel, with "Toolbox" printed at the top.

Physical Setting

Any typical training setting.

Process

1. Choose concepts and skills that are most important to the program being presented. Prior to the training program, write each concept or skill on a 3" x 5" index card. Keep it simple. Use only one or two words on each card. If there are fewer key concepts or skills than participants, duplicate some of the cards, so that each participant will receive at least one card.

2. Distribute the cards among participants as the session begins.

3. Post a flip-chart sheet labeled "Toolbox" near the front of the room and place masking tape near the flip-chart sheet.

4. At the start of the program, explain that each time a concept or skill is covered, the participant who has the card for that concept or skill should tape the card to the "toolbox."

5. At the end of the session, take the cards off the sheet one at a time and read them. Ask the participants to summarize briefly each of the concepts or skills written on the cards and then discuss it briefly.

Variations

- If a program lasts more than one day or consists of multiple modules, this technique can be used to review the material covered on a previous day or in another module before starting the new material.

- Colored cards can be used to indicate similar or related concepts, tools, or skills.

- Instead of a large-group review, divide the participants into subgroups and distribute the cards among the groups. Ask each group to prepare a short summary of each concept or skill.

Submitted by Jeanne L. Engle.

Jeanne L. Engle is an independent training, organization, and career-development consultant. Ms. Engle presents training programs in the areas of communication, management development, quality improvement, team building, and career management for business and industry, government, and nonprofit groups.

628. Apple of Your Eye: Ensuring Consistent Assessment

Goals

- To recognize that without mutually agreed-on criteria and standards, assessment results will vary widely.

- To discuss the importance of using specific criteria for performance assessment or feedback on performance.

Group Size

Ten to twenty participants divided into three subgroups.

Time Required

Fifty to sixty minutes.

Materials

- Fifteen apples of varying shapes, sizes, and quality labeled as A1, A2, A3, A4, A5, B1, B2, B3, B4, B5, C1, C2, C3, C4, and C5.

- One copy of the Apple of Your Eye Work Sheet for each participant.

- A flip-chart page with pre-drawn chart for recording each group's apple ratings. The chart should include three columns, one for each subgroup, and 15 rows, one for each apple.

- Pens or pencils for participants.

- An easel and felt-tipped markers for the facilitator.

Physical Setting

A room in which the three subgroups can work without overhearing one another or breakout rooms.

Process

1. Introduce the activity, stating that it is a hands-on activity in which participants will have an opportunity to make rating decisions.

2. Give each participant a copy of the Apple of Your Eye Work Sheet and a pen or pencil.

3. Explain the background for the activity. Tell the participants:

   As a public relations effort, your company has decided to supply freshly baked apple pies for the local Chamber of Commerce 4th of July dinner. A bakery has been hired to make the apple pies. However, because the quality of pies is linked to the company's image, company leaders have decided that company employees must take responsibility for selecting the apples to be baked in the pies. The apples have been purchased wholesale, and you have been chosen to be on the "Apple Selection Committee." Committee members will sort the apples into three groups:

   - "I" for apples for the pies.

   - "II" for apples for the local Homeless Food Basket.

   - "III" for apples to be discarded.

4. Have the participants form three subgroups. Direct the subgroups to work in different corners of the room (or in breakout rooms). Tell each subgroup to develop at least four criteria they will use to rate the apples. Each subgroup will receive one set of five apples at a time. They must rate each apple in each of the sets against the criteria they have developed. Explain also that during the rating process, apples can be held, measured, and examined. However, they cannot be bitten into or broken. Tell the subgroups they have five minutes to develop their lists of criteria. (Ten minutes.)

5. Provide one set of five apples to each subgroup. Tell the subgroups they will have five minutes to rate each set of apples. After five minutes, pass the sets of apples to another group to rate. Again, after five minutes, pass the final set of apples to each subgroup. (Fifteen minutes.)

6. Reconvene the large group. Have each subgroup report their ratings for each of the fifteen apples. Write the results on the prepared flip-chart sheet.

7. Compare and discuss the results of the rating with questions such as the following:

- How many apples were rated the same by all of the subgroups? What percentage was this? What was the percentage of disagreement?

- What criteria did the different subgroups use? How many criteria were similar? How many criteria were unique to one subgroup?

- How did your subgroup decide on its criteria for rating apples? Was there disagreement within your subgroup on the criteria?

- Was there disagreement within your subgroup on specific ratings? How did you resolve those differences?

- How is this rating exercise similar to employee performance, feedback assessments, or other situations on the job?

- What can you do to ensure that different individuals are more likely to agree on a performance or material assessment? At what point in time should criteria be set?

(Fifteen to twenty-five minutes.)

Variations

- Before the session, identify four criteria for evaluating the apples, then rate the apples yourself. At the completion of the subgroup ratings, provide your ratings as the "correct" answers against which to compare each subgroup's ratings. The subgroup that has the greatest number of matches with your ratings is the "winner." The purpose of adding this dimension is two-fold:

    - To add a competitive element for fun.

    - To reinforce the fact that an assessment can be perceived as highly arbitrary when criteria are not agreed on ahead of time by all those involved.

    If this dimension is added, do not provide a significant reward for "winning." Also, be sure the session includes other activities in which "losing" groups may have a chance to win.

- Instead of apples, the same activity can be done using any other type of readily available and inexpensive object. Depending on the business of your organization, it may be appropriate to choose another type of produce, or even a manufactured object, and modify the task to reflect a typical activity in which your organization engages. The key is to choose an object to rate that will vary widely from sample to sample.

- If the group is small (five or fewer participants), this activity can be conducted by having each person rate the apples individually. In making this modification, you lose the group interaction and consensus building required to develop rating criteria and to agree on the ratings. However, you will still obtain the same outcome: Apples will be rated differently by different individuals.

Submitted by Catherine Hayden.

Catherine Hayden *is a partner in Hayden Carmichael Training, a custom training design company. Ms. Hayden has developed custom training programs for Fortune 500 companies in the areas of management, sales, customer service, technical, and job-specific skills. She has worked in a variety of training media, including video, computer-based training, and desktop multimedia.*

APPLE OF YOUR EYE WORK SHEET

Instructions: As a public relations effort, your company has decided to supply freshly baked apple pies for the local Chamber of Commerce 4th of July dinner. A bakery has been hired to make the apple pies. However, because the quality of pies is linked to your company's image, it has been decided that the company itself must take responsibility for selecting the apples to be used in the pies. The apples have been purchased wholesale and you have been selected as a member of the "Apple Selection Committee."

As a group, you must establish at least four criteria for selecting the apples, based on a visual and hand inspection. You may not poke, prod, or bite the apples or damage them in any way. Be sure the criteria you use are appropriate for apple pies. Based on your criteria, place each apple into one of the following categories:

I = Acceptable for apple pies at the Chamber of Commerce dinner

II = Acceptable for the Homeless Food Basket

III = To be discarded

Identify your group's criteria for choosing apples and list them below. Then, as a group, come to an agreement on a rating for each apple in each of the sets.

Criteria:

1. _____

   _____

2. _____

   _____

3. _____

   _____

4. _____

   _____

Apple Ratings:

Set A	Set B	Set C
A–1	B–1	C–1
A–2	B–2	C–2
A–3	B–3	C–3
A–4	B–4	C–4
A–5	B–5	C–5

629. MANAGEMENT-HR PARTNERING: STRATEGIC HR ISSUES

Goals

- To increase awareness of strategic human resource (HR) issues.

- To provide the participants with an opportunity to discuss organizational responses to strategic HR issues.

- To help the participants to plan appropriate individual responses to strategic HR issues.

Group Size

A minimum of two groups of three members each. A maximum of sixteen participants, in groups of three or four members each. Participants should be supervisory personnel and higher (from the same organization) who have one or more direct reports.

Time Required

One and one-half to two hours.

Materials

- One copy of the Management-HR Partnering Strategic HR Issues and Responses Work Sheet for each participant.

- A pen or pencil for each participant.

- Two or three pieces of flip-chart paper and two different colors of felt-tipped markers for each subgroup.

- One of the organization's HR policy manuals for each subgroup.

- A flip chart and markers for the facilitator.

- Masking tape.

Physical Setting

A room large enough for the subgroups to sit at small tables or in a circle of chairs for discussion without disturbing other subgroups. There must be plenty of wall space for posting the flip-chart paper.

Process

1. Introduce the activity with a short discussion of supervisory responsibilities in the area of human resources. A good way to begin the discussion is to ask the participants, "What are the best ways to partner with your company's Human Resources Department to get the best efforts from employees?" (It is important to emphasize the partnering aspects to create positive results.) (Five minutes.)

2. Distribute a copy of the Management-HR Partnering Strategic HR Issues and Responses Work Sheet to every participant. Select one of the issues from the work sheet and ask the group for the main considerations in that issue for their organization. Post their comments down the left-hand side of the flip chart. Then ask how managers and supervisors need to respond to each item. List each response next to the main consideration. (Five minutes.)

3. Tell the participants to fill out their individual work sheets following your example. (Twenty minutes.)

4. Have the participants assemble into subgroups of three or four members each. Give each subgroup flip-chart paper and felt-tipped markers. Provide each subgroup with a copy of the organization's HR policy manual for reference. Explain that the subgroups should discuss the main considerations and responses for each issue, using the notes that individuals have completed on their work sheets. Tell the subgroups that they must reach agreement about the five main considerations and the responses for each. As the subgroups work, circulate among them, offering assistance as needed. (Thirty minutes.)

5. Reconvene the total group and ask each subgroup to post its work and present it to the total group, in turn. (Five to eight minutes per small group.)

6. Lead a concluding discussion based on questions such as the following:

   ■ How aware are supervisors and managers in your organization of strategic HR issues?

- How well do you believe that supervisors and managers in your organization are handling strategic HR issues?

- What knowledge have you gained about appropriate responses to strategic HR issues?

- What HR issues need to be addressed more in your workplace?

- How could this occur?

- What support would you need?

- Does your HR department solicit/welcome input, feedback, and co-operation from supervisors and managers?

- If not, why not?

- How will you incorporate what you learned from this session to strengthen your partnership with the HR department?

(Fifteen minutes to one-half hour.)

Variations

- The issues on the work sheet can be changed to be more specific to the organization.

- The activity can be completed in a different setting, using group-decision support software.

- The activity can be part of a SWOT analysis during strategic planning.

- The activity can be incorporated into a supervisory-training program.

- The activity can be part of a data-collection effort to determine the impact of organizational HR practices.

Submitted by Robert C. Preziosi.

Robert C. Preziosi, D.P.A., is a professor of management education in the School of Business and Entrepreneurship at Nova Southeastern University in Fort Lauderdale, Florida. In 1997, he received the school's first Excellence in Teaching Award. He also is president of Management Associates, a consulting firm. He has worked as a human resources director, a line manager, and a leadership-training administrator. As a trainer, his areas of interest include leadership, adult learning, and all aspects of management and executive development. In 1984 he was given the Outstanding Contribution to HRD Award by ASTD and in 1996 he received his second ASTD Torch Award.

MANAGEMENT-HR PARTNERING STRATEGIC HR ISSUES AND RESPONSES WORK SHEET

Issue	Response

1. Health care costs

_____

_____

_____

_____

2. Workplace violence

_____

_____

_____

_____

3. Gender equity

_____

_____

_____

_____

4. Labor availability

_____

_____

_____

_____

5. Skill retooling

_____

_____

_____

_____

6. Workplace democracy

_____

_____

_____

_____

Issue	Response
7. Pay for performance	_____
	_____
	_____
	_____
8. Workplace efficiency	_____
	_____
	_____
	_____
9. Workforce mental health	_____
	_____
	_____
	_____
10. Telecommuting	_____
	_____
	_____
	_____
11. Leadership renewal	_____
	_____
	_____
	_____
12. Worker diversity	_____
	_____
	_____
	_____

630. Rope-a-Leader:
Experiencing the Emergence of Leadership

Goals

- To provide the participants with the opportunity to experience and observe the emergence of leadership within a group.

- To discuss the emergence of leadership.

Group Size

Twenty to thirty-five participants in subgroups of five or seven.

Time Required

Forty minutes.

Materials

- Twenty-five feet of ¼-inch rope, twine, or macramé cord for each subgroup.

Physical Setting

Any area large enough so that all the subgroups can work on the floor without disturbing one another.

Process

1. Ask the participants to assemble in subgroups of five or seven. (Odd numbers work best.) Once subgroups have assembled, place a rope on the floor near each group. (*Note:* You may place ropes in several locations prior to beginning this activity.) (Five minutes.)

2. Explain that the task of each subgroup is to use the rope to form "an absolutely perfect" circle on the floor. When finished, the rope should lie on

the floor with no one touching it to hold it in place. Tell participants they may *not* talk to one another or to you during the activity and that you will be the final judge as to when they have accomplished the task. Tell them to begin, giving them no more than two or three minutes.

3. While subgroups are completing the task, walk around from subgroup to subgroup "judging" their work and being critical about the final shapes they have created.

4. After the circles have been completed, tell the subgroups to form a perfect square, then a triangle, a trapezoid, and an octagon. Remind the participants not to talk. (Ten minutes.)

5. After all of the shapes have been completed say, "On the count of 3, point to the leader of your subgroup. Ready? 1, 2, 3." Ask members of each subgroup, in turn, how they selected that particular leader.

6. Reconvene the large group and lead a discussion based on the following questions:

   ■ How did the leadership evolve in your group?

   ■ How did other members of the group acquiesce to the leadership?

   ■ Did conflict occur in any groups? Why or why not?

   ■ How does what happened here compare to what happens in a typical work setting at your organization?

   (Fifteen minutes.)

Variations

■ This activity can be used for team building.

■ At the end of the activity, the group can discuss what attributes of the leaders made the process work. List the attributes on a flip chart for a further discussion of leadership.

Submitted by John W. Peterson and Sherry R. Mills.

John W. Peterson and Sherry R. Mills are the founders and partners in Creative Training & Conference Management, Colorado Springs, Colorado. Both have master's degrees in education and have developed and presented workshops on a variety of topics throughout the United States, including several presentations at

ASTD national leadership, chapter management, and regional conferences. They specialize in training for nonprofit organizations. Ms. Mills is a past president of the Pikes Peak chapter of ASTD and Mr. Peterson has served on the board of directors. Both have served on the Management and Assessment Program (MAP) for ASTD nationally.

I ntroduction
to the Inventories, Questionnaires, and Surveys Section

Inventories, questionnaires, and surveys are important tools to the HRD professional. It may be difficult for participants and clients to look at themselves objectively. These feedback tools help respondents take stock of themselves and their organizations and understand how a particular theory applies to them or to their situations.

These instruments—inventories, questionnaires, and surveys—are useful in a number of training and consulting situations: privately for self-diagnosis; one-on-one to plan individual development; in a small group to open discussion; in a work team to help the team to focus on its highest priorities; or in an organization to gather data to achieve progress.

You will find that the use of inventories, questionnaires, and surveys enriches, personalizes, and deepens training, development, and intervention designs. Many can be combined with other experiential learning activities or articles in this or other *Annuals* to design an exciting, involving, practical, and well-rounded intervention.

Each instrument includes the background necessary for understanding, presenting, and using it. Interpretive information, scales, and scoring sheets are also provided. In addition, we include the reliability and validity data contributed by the authors. If you wish additional information on any of these instruments, contact the authors directly. You will find their addresses and telephone numbers in the "Contributors" listing near the end of this volume.

Other assessment tools that address a wider variety of topics can be found by using our comprehensive *Reference Guide to Handbooks and Annuals*. This guide indexes all the instruments that we have published to date in the *Annuals*. You will find this complete, up-to-date, and easy-to-use resource valuable for locating other instruments, as well as for locating experiential learning activities and articles.

The 1999 Annual: Volume 1, Training includes three assessment tools in the following categories:

Communication

Supervisor Selection: The Supervisory Assessment Instrument
by Philip Benham

Consulting and Facilitating

The Perception of Empowerment Instrument (PEI)
by W. Kirk Roller

Leadership

The Leadership Dimensions Survey by Gerald V. Miller

SUPERVISOR SELECTION:
THE SUPERVISORY ASSESSMENT INSTRUMENT

Philip Benham

Abstract: In too many cases, senior managers look back at their decisions to promote others to management with regret. Many managers are not competent and contaminate their organizations with uninspired leadership and inefficient administration. This instrument addresses a major cause of poor performance by managers: the criteria used to promote people into managerial positions in the first place.

The Supervisory Assessment Instrument (SAI) assesses three competencies essential to managerial performance: technical skills, interpersonal skills, and conceptual skills. Assessors rate prospects for supervisory positions on twenty items, measuring observed proficiency in each skill area. The results indicate a prospect's readiness to assume a supervisory position.

In addition to assessing a prospect's readiness, the instrument can be used to determine training and development needs for prospective managers. It can also be used in orientation programs to explain performance expectations of supervisors. Finally, the instrument can be used to design a performance appraisal system appropriate to managerial work.

$\mathbf{A}$dvancing from a nonsupervisory position to supervisor is often a difficult transition. The conventional wisdom that the best predictor of future success is past success is useless in this situation. Past success in nonsupervisory positions has important but limited value in predicting how well someone will perform as a supervisor. Managerial work is different from nonmanagerial work (Heisler & Benham, 1992; Katz, 1974; McCall, Lombardo, & Morrison, 1988; Mintzberg, 1972).

Nonsupervisory work is largely technical in nature. It requires proficiency with tools and equipment and in performing task procedures with consistent accuracy. To a lesser extent, nonsupervisory work requires interpersonal skills—the ability to work effectively with others as a co-worker. Conceptual skills—the ability to reason in the abstract and envision the larger context in which one's job is performed—also play a role in nonsupervisory work.

On the other hand, supervisory work requires a more astute understanding of human behavior and a much higher level of proficiency in interpersonal skills. The competencies in this area range from effective listening to providing constructive feedback on performance. Maintaining one's composure with difficult people while confronting them candidly on matters that may require discipline are part of the interpersonal skill set required. Avoiding unpleasant people whose behavior is disrupting the work team or production crew and detracting from work quality is not an option for an effective supervisor.

Supervisory work also requires a growing awareness of and proficiency in conceptual thinking—the ability to analyze unstructured situations and to interpret information needed for effective decision making. Complexity and ambiguity, in other words, define much of the nature of managerial work and many of the demands made of managers. Anyone who has conducted annual performance review feedback sessions with employees who differ in talents and personalities understands this point well.

To increase our confidence in selecting the best prospects for supervision, we need to use criteria that provide better measures of the demands of supervisory work. The Supervisory Assessment Instrument provides relevant criteria to make these measurements.

DESCRIPTION OF THE INSTRUMENT

The Supervisory Assessment Instrument is designed to be used by experienced supervisors and upper level managers to assess the readiness of employees to become supervisors. The twenty items in the SAI provide measures on the three competencies—technical, interpersonal, and conceptual skills—that are essential for effective supervisory performance. Each item is scored on a four-point scale indicating the extent or frequency with which the skill is observed.

Validity

The items in the instrument are derived from research and from practical applications in several organizations. Construct validity, therefore, is quite high. Statistical assessments of content validity and of predictive validity have not been made; however, the instrument is intended to be an action research tool rather than a rigorous model intended for empirical research and theory building.

ADMINISTRATION OF THE INSTRUMENT

Total time required to administer, score, and interpret the SAI is approximately fifteen minutes per prospect or individual being evaluated.

Each rater will need one copy of the SAI per person being evaluated. The instrument is self-scoring, and it contains all the information required to score and interpret it. Suggest that raters may wish to obtain more information from the sources listed in the references. For more in-depth discussion, see Katz (1974). Katz notes that managers rely increasingly on human (relational) and conceptual skills to perform effectively. Conversely, technical skills—proficiency with tools, equipment, and operating procedures—play a diminishing role as one progresses through the ranks of management. Katz believes that management selection methods, therefore, should rely more on relational and conceptual skills than on technical skills if they are to be valid predictors of future success.

For a more comprehensive discussion of management, the work by Kotter (1982) is very instructive. Kotter concludes that effective managers are able to set agendas, that is, know what has to be done and why, and form networks, that is, establish relationships capable of providing valuable and timely information to carry out agendas. Reasoning and interpersonal skills, therefore, are key to success in situations that are often ambiguous and more complex than those encountered in nonmanagerial work.

Finally, the work by Gardner (1990) provides an excellent discussion of the attributes of leadership important to managerial success. Gardner emphasizes the role that values play in defining effective leadership. If a management prospect does not believe that people respond favorably to managers who care about their potential to grow and develop, that prospect will probably discount people's ability to contribute and to improve. In turn, these prospects will most likely neglect their interpersonal skills and fail to appreciate the role these skills play in their performance as managers.

Introduce the Session

Note that "Past is not always prologue" when it comes to selecting first-time managers. The skills that make a good functional specialist or technician are not the skills that make a good supervisor. Say that the SAI will provide a set of selection criteria that can improve greatly the accuracy of selection decisions for first-time supervisors.

Fill Out the SAI

Give participants copies of the instrument and ask them to complete it by thinking of one of their subordinates as a prospect for becoming a supervisor and to rate this person using the SAI. After everyone has finished, ask them to total the scores for the candidates they have rated and to fill out their recommendations, then lay the instrument aside.

Summarize the Katz Model

Present a brief summary of the Technical-Interpersonal-Conceptual Skill Model introduced by Katz (1974) and elaborated on in the introductory section above. The model classifies performance skills into three categories: *technical*, emphasizing proficiency with tools, equipment, and procedures; *human or relational*, emphasizing proficiency as a listener and speaker in gaining the respect and support of others; and *conceptual*, emphasizing abstract reasoning skills such as the ability to clarify an ambiguous situation and then map out an effective course of action. The model also notes that supervisors must rely more on their relational and conceptual skills than they did previously in nonsupervisory positions. Explain that as managers progress to higher levels of authority and responsibility, moreover, they should increase their use of conceptual skills and decrease their use of technical skills to meet the changing need for abstract reasoning skills in these higher level positions. Draw the model below on a flip chart.

Performance Skills Model

Specialist Supervisor Middle Manager Executive

Conceptual

Relational

Technical

Ask for Reactions

Encourage participants to share their reactions to the model and to the instrument and the value they will have in coaching and counseling, as well as in selecting prospects to become supervisors in the future. Give everyone copies of the Guidelines for Interpreting the SAI and go through it with participants. Answer any questions they may have about the instrument and the results they have obtained, helping them to understand their results and to make employee-development plans, if appropriate.

References

Gardner, J.W. (1990). *On leadership.* New York: The Free Press.

Heisler, W.J., & Benham, P.O. (1992). The challenge of management development in North America in the 1990s. *The Journal of Management Development, 11*(2), 16–31.

Katz, R.L. (1974). The skills of an effective administrator. *Harvard Business Review,* 52(5), 90–102.

Kotter, J.P. (1982). *The general managers.* New York: The Free Press.

McCall, M.W., Lombardo, M.M., & Morrison, A.M. (1988). *The lessons of experience: How successful executives develop on the job.* Lexington, MA: Lexington.

Mintzberg, H. (1973). *The nature of managerial work.* New York: Harper & Row.

Philip Benham, Ph.D., SPHR, is director of the Graduate School of Human Resource Management and Industrial Relations at Saint Francis College, Loretto, Pennsylvania. He is also a consultant specializing in management development and has written or co-authored several articles on management development and the book, Managing Human Resource Issues *(Jossey-Bass).*

Supervisory Assessment Instrument

Philip Benham

Part I: Information About Prospect

Name of Supervisory Prospect: _____

Current Position (Title): _____

Department/Group/Section: _____

Previous Assignments and Years of Experience:

(Assignments)	(Years of Experience)
1. _____	_____
2. _____	_____
3. _____	_____

Part II: Assessment of Prospect

Directions: Using the rating scale below, place an X in the appropriate column by each numbered item to indicate the *consistency* with which the person you are rating exhibits the behavior.

Rating Scale **SA** = Strongly Agree **A** = Agree **D** = Disagree **SD** = Strongly Disagree	SA	A	D	SD
Technical Competence				
1. Interprets instructions accurately.				
2. Follows task procedures correctly.				
3. Verifies the accuracy and completeness of assigned tasks; rarely has work returned because of errors/mistakes.				
4. Uses required tools and/or equipment correctly, i.e., follows proper start-up, shut-down and/or operating procedures.				

Rating Scale **SA** = Strongly Agree **A** = Agree **D** = Disagree **SD** = Strongly Disagree	SA	A	D	SD
5. Follows administrative procedures correctly, i.e., follows proper safety, security, routing and/or documentation procedures.				
6. Writes clearly and accurately; rarely has to explain the content of written work orally.				
7. Learns new technology applications correctly.				
Interpersonal Competence				
8. Maintains composure with difficult people and in difficult situations.				
9. Gives credit to others for their accomplishments and efforts.				
10. Seeks the opinions of others and incorporates their concerns into plans and actions.				
11. Speaks clearly and confidently to others.				
12. Obtains the willing support of others for tasks requiring cooperation and teamwork.				
13. Listens respectfully to others in order to understand their positions or concerns.				
14. Disagrees with others without being rude or offensive.				
Conceptual Competence				
15. Sets appropriate priorities for work assignments.				
16. Understands the job's contribution to organizational goals.				
17. Shows the importance of continuous learning by taking the initiative to improve current skills and to learn new skills.				
18. Takes the initiative to determine a course of action when assignments are unclear or ill-defined.				

Rating Scale
SA = Strongly Agree
  A = Agree
  D = Disagree
SD = Strongly Disagree
	SA	A	D	SD

19. In handling job-related problems, demonstrates an aware-ness of the long-term implications of a course of action, i.e., avoids quick fixes or expedient solutions that may later prove to be inadequate.				
20. Shows the importance of networking as a means of learning about issues and trends outside the company by becoming involved in professional and community organizations.				
Determining Total Score				
Step 1: Total the Xs marked in each column:	__	__	__	__
Step 2: Multiply numbers in Step 1 by:	× 4	× 3	× 2	× 1
Step 3: Add column totals:	+	+	+	
Step 4: Add four column totals for aggregate score:	=			

Now use the same scoring system to determine the total score under each scale: Technical Competence, Interpersonal Competence, and Conceptual Competence.

Do Not Recommend if:

☐ Candidate excludes self from consideration.

☐ Candidate scores below:

    21 on Technical Competency Scale

    18 on Interpersonal Competency Scale

    14 on Conceptual Competency Scale

Recommend if:

☐ Candidate's aggregate score is between 53 and 60 points
(Long-Term Prospect)

☐ Candidate's aggregate score is between 61 and 70 points
(Intermediate-Term Prospect)

☐ Candidate's aggregate score is between 71 and 80 points
(Near-Term Prospect)

Developmental Needs

☐ Long-Term Prospect: Needs Skills Training in:

_____

_____

_____

_____

_____

_____

☐ Intermediate-Term Prospect: Needs Skills Training in:

_____

_____

_____

_____

_____

_____

☐ Near-Term Prospect: Needs Skills Training in:

_____

_____

_____

_____

_____

_____

☐ Evaluator's Signature: _____

Date: _____

Guidelines for Interpreting the SAI

Key Terms

Rater: The participant completing the SAI on a prospect.

Prospect: The subordinate being evaluated by the participant using the SAI.

Prospect Not Recommended

1. *Prospect Excludes Self.* Identify the reason and note whether it is circumstantial or attitudinal in nature. *Circumstantial* refers to temporary situations of a personal nature that make the timing inconvenient for the prospect. Prospects who exclude themselves for circumstantial reasons should be reconsidered for supervisory opportunities at a later time. *Attitudinal* refers to a prospect's unwillingness to become a supervisor. Some people object to the increased complexity and ambiguity of supervisory work. The discomfort caused by the complexity and ambiguity is so unsettling that it preempts any attraction that increased pay and status accompanying a promotion may have. Prospects who exclude themselves for attitudinal reasons should probably be removed from the prospect list. Unless the attitude is caused by misinformation about what is expected in a supervisory role, the person probably will not succeed as a supervisor.

2. *Prospect's Ratings Are Too Low.* If the prospect fails to obtain the minimum score in one or more competencies, note the nature and severity of the difficulty. For example, did the prospect fail in one competency or in all three? Did the prospect miss the minimum score by only one or two points? Assess the likelihood that the prospect will receive a passing score after completing remedial training and some on-the-job coaching. If the likelihood is low, the prospect should be removed from the list. If the likelihood is high, however, use the data profile from the SAI to develop a plan for remedial work. As the employee responds to the training and coaching, showing improvement in the competencies targeted for development, consider reclassifying the person as a prospect.

Prospect Recommended

1. *Long-Term Prospect.* Generally, long-term prospects (those scoring between 53 and 60 points on the SAI) need additional training and exposure to certain performance situations before they will be strong candidates for

promotion to supervisor. Normally, the time required to make the improvements will be twelve to eighteen months. Long-term prospects usually need improvement in interpersonal and conceptual skills.

2. *Intermediate-Term Prospect.* Generally, intermediate-term prospects (those scoring between 61 and 70 points on the SAI) need training in just a few skills before they will be strong candidates for promotion to supervisor. Normally, the time required to make the improvements will be six to twelve months. Intermediate-term prospects usually need improvement in their interpersonal skills.

3. *Near-Term Prospect.* Generally, near-term prospects (those scoring between 71 and 80 points on the SAI) require coaching on a limited range of techniques before being nominated for promotion to supervisor. Normally, the time required to make the improvements will be one to six months. Near-term prospects usually need improvement in coaching and counseling techniques, especially those needed to implement the organization's performance appraisal system

Developmental Needs

Although training that is experiential in nature, such as role playing, is very helpful in developing skills targeted by the SAI, selected job assignments are powerful learning opportunities that often go unrecognized by managers (see McCall, Lombardo, & Morrison for an extensive discussion of this issue). For confirmed supervisory prospects, a task force assignment can be quite helpful in developing interpersonal and conceptual skills. Consider the following example:

> An interdepartmental systems conversion task force is being formed to assure that information processing needs throughout the organization are identified and integrated into a plan that is both comprehensive in scope and compatible in design. Your department must nominate someone to serve on the task force. Terry, one of your near-term prospects for supervisor, could well serve the needs of the department with technical expertise and administrative insight. You recognize, however, that the task force is also an opportunity to develop Terry's conceptual skills.
>
> Terry shows great promise for success as a supervisor. Terry needs some exposure to situations, however, that provide insight to how the organization functions as a whole. Terry also needs to experience differences of opinion that stem largely from different types

of jobs and job demands. The task force assignment will provide the experience Terry needs to develop these conceptual insights as well as some skill in building consensus among people with different perspectives on matters of common interest. You nominate Terry, citing the reasons just mentioned.

Other Benefits of the SAI

In addition to providing a valid means for determining readiness levels among prospects for promotion to supervision, the SAI can help with the following:

1. *Compliance with EEO/AA Legislation and Guidelines.* The SAI provides a means for showing consistent treatment of employees in selection decisions. It also identifies specific needs for development and it provides a time frame for completing a developmental plan. This documentation can help avoid unexplained variances between protected and unprotected classes, as defined in the law, in promotion rates to supervision.

2. *Compliance with Americans with Disabilities Act.* The SAI provides a substantial start in compiling a list of "essential functions" required of a supervisor. Knowing these essential functions will help organizations comply with the ADA in screening prospects who are considered to be disabled. The SAI will also help identify when "reasonable accommodations" can be made for well-qualified prospects who may require an accommodation to perform the job of supervisor satisfactorily.

3. *Retention of Promising Employees.* The SAI can generate interest in the development and advancement of an organization's most promising employees. Often this interest can make the difference in keeping an employee who may resign to take a position elsewhere.

4. *Performance Appraisal.* The SAI provides a way to use job-related behavior as a basis for evaluating supervisory performance. It also provides consistency between criteria used to select people for supervisory positions and criteria used subsequently to evaluate actual job performance. This consistency will help reinforce the importance of these behaviors to both the managers making the evaluations and the supervisors being evaluated.

Reference

McCall, M.W., Lombardo, M.M., & Morrison, A.M. (1988). *The lessons of experience: How successful executives develop on the job.* Lexington, MA: Lexington.

THE PERCEPTION OF EMPOWERMENT INSTRUMENT (PEI)

W. Kirk Roller

Abstract: Attempts to identify the specific individual components or dimensions of empowerment and to develop measurement tools for these specific dimensions have only begun recently. The Perception of Empowerment Instrument (PEI) measures the empowerment dimensions of autonomy, responsibility, and participation. The dimensions measured by the instrument are more behaviorally specific than those measured in any previous scale. Respondents rate their level of agreement with fifteen items that describe the presence of the three dimensions in their work environments. The scale can be used to compare individuals within groups or groups within organizations to identify individual perceptions and areas for organizational intervention and development.

INTRODUCTION

The concept of employee empowerment is addressed frequently in the literature on organizational communication, organizational behavior, organization theory, organization development, and management and is of significant interest to organizational and management researchers and practitioners. Despite all the attention given employee empowerment by both the academic and popular media—and by organizations themselves—there is little agreement among either scholars or practitioners as to the exact nature of empowerment. There is no generally accepted definition of empowerment and, consequently, no commonly accepted method to measure it.

Concepts that cannot be measured directly in a real setting are referred to as "theoretical constructs." Empowerment is such a theoretical construct. It cannot be measured directly, but only through the observation of related phenomena. It is important that theoretical concepts be related to sensory impressions in concrete situations. An effective and useful assessment scale measures a construct by assessing specific behaviors that are inferred from the content of the construct. The Perception of Empowerment Instrument measures specific behaviors that have been associated with individual empowerment.

Any measure of a construct may represent part of a broader measure of the same construct. The three dimensions measured by the Perception of Empowerment Instrument are more concrete and behaviorally specific representations of generally recognized dimensions of empowerment. By gaining a clearer understanding of these empowerment dimensions and of how to measure them in individual employees, scholars and practitioners will be able to design effective organizational strategies and structures that support the development of empowering and empowered organizational cultures.

Consultants, researchers, and practitioners who want to use the Perception of Empowerment Instrument as an assessment tool should possess a thorough understanding about the role of empowerment in the workplace in order to provide context and effective processing of individual and aggregate scores.

DESCRIPTION OF THE INSTRUMENT

The instrument is composed of fifteen items measuring the dimensions of autonomy, participation, and responsibility. Participants respond using a five-point scale. Participants can self-score their surveys by following the directions on the scoring sheet. An interpretation sheet is provided. A duplicate scoring sheet is also returned to the facilitator for the collection and determination of aggregate scores.

Reliability

A test can be described as reliable if it is self-consistent and yields the same score for each respondent (assuming that the respondents have not changed) on retesting. The first measure of reliability described is referred to as internal-consistency reliability and the second is referred to as test-retest reliability.

Internal-consistency reliability estimates were obtained for the PEI by computing Cronbach's alpha for the responses to the items that measure each of the three empowerment dimensions. The items in the *autonomy* dimension displayed an internal-consistency estimate of .796. The items in the *responsibility* dimension showed an internal consistency estimate of .803. Analysis of items in the *participation* dimension revealed an internal consistency estimate of .866.

The test-retest reliability of the PEI instrument was determined by calculating the correlation between paired response sets. The correlation between average scores from the paired response sets was .746.

Validity

Content validity refers to how well an instrument captures what is being "tested." Content validity can be evaluated subjectively by experts in the field of interest. In this case, four experts in the area of empowerment were asked to evaluate the content validity of the PEI. All strongly agreed that the items in the instrument satisfactorily assess each of the dimensions. The internal-consistency reliability demonstrated by the instrument also indicates that the items in the instrument reflect the same behavioral domain.

Criterion-related validity refers to the extent to which a measure demonstrates a correlation with some external indicator of the same attribute. A significant correlation has been demonstrated between responses to the PEI and a previously validated empowerment instrument (Spreitzer, 1993) that measures related dimensions. The correlation between average scores on the PEI and average scores on the criterion scale was .816.

Theory Behind the Instrument

The empowerment construct has been examined and applied in a broad variety of contexts. Various scholars adopting diverse perspectives have viewed the nature of the construct differently. A growing body of research indicates certain common dimensions of the empowerment construct. Three dimensions that appear to be particularly important relate to autonomy (individual perceptions of self-control), participation (control over one's environment), and responsibility (personal commitment). These three dimensions are discussed below.

Autonomy

A common dimension evident in prior research on individual empowerment has been described as an individual's perception of being in control or "autonomy." When empowerment is viewed this way, it is seen as the process by which a leader or manager delegates or shares power or control over resources and individuals. Power is seen as the basic element of empowerment.

This common description of empowerment as the simple delegation of authority and control to subordinates does not address important questions regarding the way individuals experience empowerment. Empowerment is much more complex than the simple sharing or shifting of authority. Power, from the empowered employee's point of view, is internal to individuals. It addresses their perceptions of their own abilities to deal successfully with the challenges they face. It is not the power to dominate but the power to accomplish. This power is the intrinsic need for self-determination and self-efficacy.

Empowerment from the management perspective is the process of enabling individuals to feel empowered by increasing their levels of perceived self-efficacy through increased self-determination. "Autonomy," as measured by the Perception of Empowerment Instrument, refers to an individual's perception of the level of freedom and personal control that he or she possesses and is able to exercise in the performance of his or her job.

Participation

Individual participation in organizational decision making is an important dimension of individual empowerment. Employees cannot feel empowered unless they are encouraged to participate fully in developing and improving organizational processes.

The "participation" dimension of the PEI measures individuals' perceptions of their influence in producing desired effects in their environments, the degree to which they feel that they have input into their organization's administrative or strategic decisions or processes beyond their specific job requirements.

Responsibility

Empowered employees exhibit commitment, ownership, and responsibility regarding the jobs they do and the outcomes of the decisions they make. Organizational members in an empowered organization, provided with increased autonomy, participation, and access to information and knowledge, will respond with increased commitment and effectiveness. The "responsibility" dimension of the PEI is related to the level of concern, care, or responsibility that an individual brings to a task or position and to a feeling of psychological investment in the results that produces commitment and energy.

ADMINISTRATION OF THE INSTRUMENT

Do not discuss the concept of empowerment prior to administering the survey. Tell the participants that the survey measures certain attributes that are important in modern organizations and that the findings will be discussed when the survey has been completed. Inform the participants that all responses to the survey will be confidential and that any scores revealed to the entire group will represent group averages only. Give each participant a copy of the PEI Survey and give them about fifteen minutes to complete it.

THE SCORING PROCESS

After the participants have completed the Survey, hand out two copies of the PEI Scoring Sheet to each person and have participants follow the steps below. The scoring process takes ten to fifteen minutes.

1. Have participants transfer their responses from the Survey to the appropriate spaces in Section 1 on the PEI Scoring Sheet.

2. Tell the participants to total their responses for each of the three dimensions and to record the sums as the Dimension Totals.

3. Next, have them divide each Dimension Total by the number of items to find the Dimension Average and transfer their Dimension *Totals* to Section 2.

4. Now have them add the three Total scores in Section 2 to find their Scale Totals and write that number in the appropriate box.

5. After they have completed Section 2, they should transfer their Scale Totals to Section 3 and divide the scale total by the number of scale items (3) to find their Average Item Scores.

6. Finally, have them transfer their numbers onto the second PEI Scoring Sheet that you handed out. Collect the duplicate PEI Scoring Sheets and use them to determine the group's average overall item scores and, if possible, the group's average item scores for each dimension. Post them on a flip chart in the same format as the PEI Interpretation Sheet. While you are doing this, you may wish to have the participants take a short break.

HELPING PARTICIPANTS INTERPRET THEIR SCORES

Hand out copies of the PEI Interpretation Sheet. Ask the participants to record their individual scores in the spaces provided and to write in the aggregate scores that you have written on the flip chart. Review the definitions of each empowerment dimension from the PEI Interpretation Sheet and ask the participants to look for patterns in their own scores compared with the aggregate group scores. Lead a discussion on the relevance that variations from the mean score may have for individuals. Ask open-ended questions that promote dialogue within the group regarding the meaning of the scores. Solicit individual suggestions regarding how this information can be used to formulate action plans that will improve individual and/or organizational effectiveness.

Define empowerment in terms of the three empowerment dimensions described above and on the PEI Interpretation Sheet and briefly discuss the relevance of empowerment in organizational environments. Focus on ways that participants can increase their individual and organizational effectiveness.

OTHER USES FOR THE INSTRUMENT

Although the instrument was designed primarily to generate dialogue, inquiry, and action planning within intact groups, it also can be used to examine variations between intact groups or teams or within or between organizations.

Reference

Spreitzer, G.M. (1993). *Psychological improvement in the workplace: Construct definition, measurement, and validation.* Los Angeles: University of Southern California.

W. Kirk Roller, Ph.D., is an independent consultant with extensive experience as a professional manager, consultant, instructor, facilitator, and trainer. He is an expert in change management, organizational design and development, interpersonal and organizational communication, systems thinking, small group facilitation, team building, and experiential training.

PEI Survey

W. Kirk Roller

Instructions: Circle the number that describes your reaction to each of the statements below.

5 = Strongly Agree   4 = Agree   3 = Neutral   2 = Disagree   1 = Strongly Disagree

Item		Response			
1. I have the freedom to decide how to do my job.	5	4	3	2	1
2. I am often involved when job changes are planned.	5	4	3	2	1
3. I can be creative in finding solutions to problems on the job.	5	4	3	2	1
4. I am involved in determining organizational goals.	5	4	3	2	1
5. I am responsible for the results of my own decisions on the job.	5	4	3	2	1
6. My input is solicited in planning changes.	5	4	3	2	1
7. I take responsibility for what I do on the job.	5	4	3	2	1
8. I am responsible for the outcomes of my actions on the job.	5	4	3	2	1
9. I have a lot of autonomy in my job.	5	4	3	2	1
10. I am personally responsible for the work I do.	5	4	3	2	1
11. I am involved in decisions that affect me on the job.	5	4	3	2	1
12. I make my own decisions about how to do my work.	5	4	3	2	1
13. I am my own boss most of the time.	5	4	3	2	1
14. I am involved in creating our vision of the future.	5	4	3	2	1
15. My ideas and inputs are valued at work.	5	4	3	2	1

PEI Scoring Sheet

Instructions:

1. Transfer your responses from the PEI Survey to the appropriate spaces in Section 1 below.

2. Add your responses for each dimension and record the number as the Dimension Total.

3. Divide the Dimension Total as shown to find the Dimension Average.

4. Copy your Dimension Totals to Section 2.

5. Add your Dimension Totals together to find your Scale Total.

6. Transfer the Scale Total to Section 3.

7. Divide the Scale Total by 3 to find your Average Item Score.

Section 1					
Dimension 1		Dimension 2		Dimension 3	
Item #	Response	Item #	Response	Item #	Response
1		2		5	
3		4		7	
9		6		8	
12		11		10	
13		14			
		15			
Dimension Total		Dimension Total		Dimension Total	
Dimension Average (Total/5)		Dimension Average (Total/6)		Dimension Average (Total/4)	

Section 2						
Total 1		Total 2		Total 3		Scale Total
	+		+		=	

Section 3		
Scale Total/3		Average Item Score
	=	

When you have finished your PEI Scoring Sheet, copy your numbers onto the duplicate Scoring Sheet you received and give it to the facilitator.

PEI Interpretation Sheet

Instructions: Record your scores and the group's scores provided by the facilitator in the spaces provided. Generally, if you received a higher score than the group average, it indicates a strength in that dimension. Look for patterns in your scores relative to the group scores.

Keep the following definitions in mind as you study your scores in relation to the group average:

- *Autonomy (Dimension 1):* An individual's perception of the level of freedom and personal control that he or she possesses and is able to exercise in the performance of his or her job.

- *Participation (Dimension 2):* The degree to which an individual feels that he or she has input into his or her organization's administrative or strategic decisions, that is, the individual's perceived influence in organizational decisions and processes beyond his or her specific job requirements.

- *Responsibility (Dimension 3):* The level of concern, care, commitment, or responsibility that an individual brings to a task or position and the feeling of psychological investment that produces commitment and energy.

Result	Self	Group
Scale Total		
Average Item Score		
Average Score Dimension 1 (Autonomy)		
Average Score Dimension 2 (Participation)		
Average Score Dimension 3 (Responsibility)		

The Leadership Dimensions Survey

Gerald V. Miller

Abstract: The Leadership Dimensions Survey is a tool
to assist those on the odyssey of leadership. The survey is based on four leadership competencies: profound knowledge, profound strategy, purposeful
direction, and purposeful behaviors. These four
competencies, when paired on a grid, yield four leadership dimensions or "virtues": constancy of purpose,
congruity of activity, competency of outcome, and
compatibility of values. The four competencies, as
measured by the Leadership Dimensions Survey, allow for the generation and sustenance of trust between leader and follower, which forms the basis for
a work environment that is both productive and able
to adapt to and thrive in a changing and complex
business world.

The Leadership Dimensions Survey can be used
for self-discovery, leadership development, coaching in human dimensions of leadership, and other
leadership applications.

REFRAMING LEADERSHIP

In a world of unceasing change, downsizing, reinventing, reengineering, business process redesign, customer focus, and high-performance teams, the business leader of today must balance the tremendous demands of managing that change and complexity with work output and productivity. Those leaders who operate on the 19th Century model of bureaucracy, a model based on words and actions, of control and order, are not going to pass muster in the next millennium.

Successful business leaders have mastered a new set of knowledge, skills, and attitudes with which to face the challenges of corporate reality—in effect, a completely new form of leadership. This form of leadership is observable and learnable. Given the opportunity to learn, receive feedback, and practice, those who desire to lead and improve their ability to lead can do so.

LEADERSHIP COMPETENCIES AND DIMENSIONS

Today's leaders must think in terms of a leadership system, seeing a framework of patterns and interrelationships. Unfortunately, we usually focus on isolated parts instead of seeing the whole system of leadership, and then we wonder why our efforts at solving problems or perpetuating successes fail.

It is especially important to see the world of leadership as a whole system as it continues to grow more complex. Complexity can overwhelm and undermine our efforts if we do not have a model or a system to guide our efforts. A model helps us see the patterns that lie behind events and details, which can simplify the art of leadership.

The leadership systems model is based on four interrelated competencies:

- Profound knowledge,

- Profound strategy,

- Purposeful direction, and

- Purposeful behaviors.

These competencies can be visualized on an interconnecting axis, as shown in Figure 1.

The word "profound" connotes something deep-seated. To be profound is to go beyond the surface, beneath the veneer issues to what is the true essence of something. It requires an intellectual depth and insight. Perhaps you can remember a time when you were conversing with someone who said something profound. It took the conversation to a new depth.

Profound knowledge is a necessary competency that ensures a basis of information, experience, expertise, and data. To possess profound knowledge is to possess something beyond mere perceptions.

Profound strategy indicates a well-thought-out plan or course of action that goes beyond the status quo. It is the insightful art of development of the exceptional blueprint or scheme.

To be "purposeful" is to be, literally, full of purpose. To be purposeful is to be meaningful. It is acting with thoughtful intention, not out of convenience. It requires resolution and determination. When one is purposeful, one has an aim or goal, a reason for behaving in a particular manner.

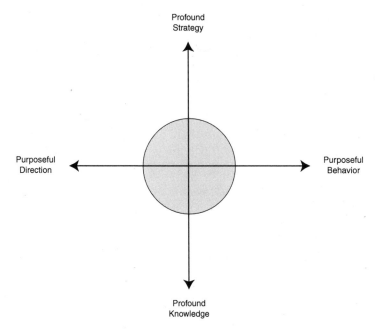

Figure 1. Competencies Axis

Purposeful direction implies that there is a vision, goal, and mission that will result in a desired future state uniquely different from the present state.

Purposeful behavior indicates that the leader's behaviors are, in fact, meaningful and are, on some level, inextricably attached to a vision or goal. The behaviors provide a role model for the values and skills needed to achieve a desired state.

THE ROLE OF TRUST IN LEADERSHIP

Leadership is not just about leaders; it is also about followers. Successful leadership depends far more on the followers' perception of the leader than on any other factor. It is a reciprocal process, occurring between people. Followers, not the leader, determine when someone possesses the qualities of leadership.

People would rather follow, and confer leadership on, individuals they can count on—even when they disagree with their viewpoints—rather than people they agree with but who shift positions frequently. Everything effective leaders do is congruent with their values, their viewpoints. The four leadership dimensions of constancy of purpose, congruity of activity, competency of outcome, and compatibility of values are realized through consistent behavior over time. This behavior is the basis of trust for followers who buy into the vision, the shared goals, and objectives and then confer leadership. Each of the four leadership dimensions takes time to generate and sustain. The result is trust.

DIMENSIONS OF LEADERSHIP

When we put the four competencies—profound knowledge, profound strategy, profound direction, and purposeful behavior—together, we form a grid with four quadrants, as seen in Figure 2. Each of these quadrants represents a leadership dimension: I: Constancy of purpose, II: Congruity of activity, III: Competency of outcome, and IV: Compatibility of values. It is these four dimensions that can be used to measure leadership proficiency.

I. Constancy of Purpose

Constancy of purpose is steadfastness, continued unwavering focus on the vision, "keeping one's eye on the prize." Purposeful direction and profound strategy make up this dimension of leadership, allowing for the development

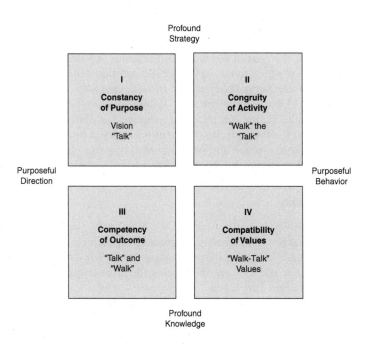

Figure 2. Dimensions of Leadership

of basic trust between leader and follower, derived from a meaningfully communicated vision and strategy.

Trust requires repeated interactions between leaders and followers and begins with vision. In nurturing an environment in which people are aware of the vision, of what is important and why it is critical, the leader creates meaning. With meaning comes trust.

Meaning also emerges from concepts, words endowed with relevance and purpose. Words are powerful. The leader, therefore, must have a "talk" to nurture the vision-oriented environment. The leader must consistently state and restate the vision in a meaningful, purposeful way that encourages people to enroll for the duration. The vision must inspire. It must articulate passion. Speaking with passion, leaders light fires under others. When the leader is a "wet match," there are no sparks to ignite passion in others and the vision is set inside. It is the role of the leader to ensure that people know and buy in to the vision.

The leader helps define the vision (purposeful direction) and "talks the talk," laying the foundation for the development of trust between the leader and the followers. The fulfillment of the vision, by definition, implies a change from the state in which we are to the state in which we want to be. This understanding on the part of the leader is the result of a well-thought-out plan and a course of action that goes beyond the status quo, the insightful art of developing the exceptional blueprint or scheme, the profound strategy.

Constancy of purpose occurs when followers believe that the leader has clear and specific reasons for initiating a change; has a clear and specific outcome in mind; understands the resources necessary to put changes into effect; understands the scope and organizational impact of a change; and understands the human impact of the change.

II. Congruity of Activity

Congruity of activity is the ability to match words and deeds, that is, to "practice what one preaches." Profound strategy and purposeful behaviors make up this dimension of leadership, promulgating the further development of trust between leader and follower and moving the organization and its people toward realization of the vision.

Saying one thing and doing another is perhaps the surest way to destroy trust. People are deeply concerned with congruity of word and deed. Congruity of activity is walking the talk and modeling the vision. What a leader does must be congruent with the vision. This dimension can generate a groundswell of trust from the foundation established through the first dimension, constancy of purpose.

Having established the vision and communicated a profound strategy, the leader must lead by example. If leaders ask followers to move toward a future state and observe certain values and standards in pursuit of that state, then the leaders must live by the same rules. That is exactly what we have been told countless times by exemplary leaders. Leadership does not sit in the stands and watch.

In order to fully commit themselves to the change process, members must believe that leaders themselves are fully committed. They should feel that the leaders are strongly convinced that the change must become a reality.

Congruity of activity ensures that followers will be committed to the change process. It shows that the leader will support the change, both publicly and privately; monitor change activities; reinforce the efforts of those who are to carry out the change effort; and make sacrifices to further the change effort.

III. Competency of Outcome

Competency of outcome is expressed in what one says, that is, "I've been there and I've done that." It occurs when a leader has profound knowledge and purposeful direction.

Dimensions I and II show how a leader must have a "talk" and a "walk"—constancy of purpose and congruity of activity. The next, dimension—competency of outcome—demands a "talk" and a "walk" backed up by substantive and demonstrable experience. This is leadership competence. To buy into leaders' visions, people must trust that leaders know what they are talking about and what they are doing. To instill trust, a leader must be seen as capable and effective. If people doubt the leader's abilities, they are unlikely to enlist in the change effort and pursue the vision.

Leadership competence does not necessarily refer to a leader's technical ability. Rather, people look for competency in the following areas:

- Systems thinking,
- Human side of management,
- Communication and interpersonal relationships,
- Giving and receiving feedback,
- Understanding and responding to needs of individual team members,
- One-on-one consultation (problems and individual needs),
- Team building and group dynamics,
- Employing informal power to influence team behavior and desired outcomes,
- Linking individuals, groups, and projects together across the organization, and
- Training and coaching in operational, administrative, and managerial functions.

Competency of outcome solidifies the trust developed thus far, setting the stage for the fourth dimension, compatibility of values.

IV. Compatibility of Values

Compatibility of values is the integration of what one believes, says, and does with the organizational value system, that is, "evidence of trust begets trust." It occurs when a leader has profound knowledge and purposeful behavior.

Compatibility of values manifests itself in interdependence, the necessarily shared value for effective leadership. Leaders must value and protect interdependence, rather than creating a climate of independence, dependence, or codependence. When held and employed unilaterally, interdependence creates a work environment of the highest efficiency, effectiveness, and professional and personal satisfaction.

Interdependence calls for coactive (synergistic) behaviors, consistent with the highest good of all concerned. Too often leaders encourage pure independence. Especially in the workplace, people must be interdependent. In the workplace, independence translates as adolescent, self-centered behavior. It is the role of the leader to believe in, value, and demonstrate the importance of interdependence. Figure 3 illustrates the developmental nature of interdependence.

The leader promotes an interdependent climate for team members and does not interfere unless it becomes necessary. The team members are trusted and given freedom (empowered and enabled) to plan their own ways of doing their work (the how) in accord with the leader's vision (the what and why). They are expected to solve problems and to ask for guidance only when it is needed. By providing freedom of work, encouraging initiative, and supporting experimentation and teamwork, leaders also help to satisfy the followers' needs for belonging, affection, and security.

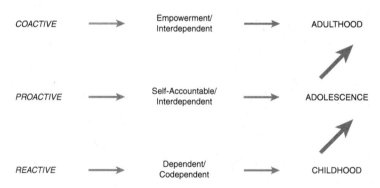

Figure 3. The Development of Interdependence

SUMMARY

Although both management and leadership are necessary to the success of any effort in today's business world, change, complexity, and continued demands for productivity and efficiency require a greater emphasis on leading. The specific knowledge, behaviors, and skills that exceptional leaders have in common, all operating under the umbrella of human systems thinking, have been identified. They are embodied in the four dimensions of leadership: constancy of purpose, congruity of activity, competency of outcome, and compatibility of values.

Proper leadership empowers and enables the individuals and teams that constitute an organization. Good leaders make team members feel that they are at the very heart of things. Followers feel that they, interdependently, make a difference to the success of the organization. This sense of empowerment can lead to increased productivity and efficiency, keys to maintaining success in a changing business world.

THE INSTRUMENT

The Leadership Dimensions Survey is designed to assess the leadership skills of aspiring, potential, or present leaders on four dimensions. The survey consists of a thirty-two-item questionnaire, a scoring sheet, an interpretation sheet that covers results on each of the four dimensions, and a Leadership Dimensions Map on which one can chart the results of his or her survey. In addition, a sample letter for participants to send to respondents and an action planning sheet are included here.

The survey is designed to be completed by five of the leader's peers, supervisors, or subordinates (the "respondents"). Each question presents a statement about the leader. Respondents are asked to mark whether they strongly agree, are inclined to agree, are inclined to disagree, or strongly disagree with the statement as it applies to the leader.

Validity and Reliability

No validity or reliability data are available on the Leadership Dimensions Survey. However, the instrument has face validity, as its purpose is to make participants more aware of their leadership behaviors through this feedback process.

Administration

The following process is suggested for facilitating a workshop on leadership with several participants. At least a week prior to working with the leaders, give each of them five copies of the Leadership Dimensions Survey and copies of the Leadership Dimensions Letter to Participants. Tell them to write letters on their own stationery similar to the sample letter to respondents, attach letters to the survey, and give them to five peers, supervisors, or subordinates, who are to follow the instructions to complete it and return it in a sealed envelope anonymously either to the leader or to you, the facilitator. (*Note:* Be sure to specify whether you are to receive the surveys or whether the leaders will collect them. An advantage of collecting them yourself is that they are less likely to be forgotten on the day of the workshop.) Anonymity allows for more candid responses. If the surveys are returned in time, they may be scored prior to the workshop, but it is important for leaders to do their own interpretation and mapping.

Scoring

The questionnaires can be scored either before or during the workshop. Both the Leadership Dimensions Scoring Sheet and Leadership Dimensions Interpretation Sheet sort the thirty-two statements by leadership dimension.

Hand out the completed Leadership Dimensions Scoring Sheets (or ask the leaders to score their own during the session) to the appropriate leader along with blank copies of the Leadership Dimensions Interpretation Sheet. If they are scoring their own surveys, tell the leaders to transfer the scores they received for each question to the A, B, C, D, and E columns on the Scoring Sheet. Each column represents one respondent. Be sure that they total the scores *horizontally* and divide by the number of responses to determine their average scores for each question, then write their scores in the "average" column. Next, tell leaders to add the averages *vertically* to obtain a total score for each dimension.

When they have finished filling out the Scoring Sheet, hand out the Leadership Dimensions Map and tell the leaders to plot their four totals in the appropriate quadrants. Draw a sample on the flip chart to show them how to map their leadership dimensions. Next, hand out Leadership Dimensions Interpretation Sheets to all leaders and ask them to study their scores. Discuss the meaning of various combinations of scores and have people share their maps and thoughts in small groups or in pairs. After everyone knows what his or her results say, hand out copies of the Leadership Dimensions Action Planning Sheet and ask leaders to make action plans to improve their leadership dimensions in the future. Ask everyone to share as appropriate.

The scoring, mapping, and interpretation of the Leadership Dimensions Survey usually requires thirty minutes to an hour to complete. The discussion phase and action planning will take another hour.

POTENTIAL USES OF THE INSTRUMENT

The Leadership Dimensions Survey is designed as a self-discovery and feedback tool. It has the following potential uses:

- As part of leadership training wherein participants have the survey completed by supervisors, peers, and subordinates prior to the training event. During the leadership training, the results can be discussed as the foundation for the workshop.

- As a coaching tool to be administered by the supervisor of someone who wishes to improve his or her leadership skills. The coach can review the results of the survey with the learner.

- As an assessment tool for future leaders. The results can form the basis of an individual leadership development plan.

- As a process intervention tool for consultants working with leaders. The results can show contributions the leaders make to the organization, point out potential pitfalls they have, and lead to suggestions for improvement and development.

- As a basis for discussion throughout an organization about the relationship between present and desired leadership styles.

- As a format for any organization that wishes to assess its readiness to implement a more effective style of leadership.

References

Bennis, W., & Nanus, B. (1986). *Leaders: The strategies for taking charge.* New York: Harper & Row.

Forkas, C.M,. & DeBacker, P. (1996). *Maximum leadership.* New York: Holt.

Hesselbein, F., Goldsmith, M., & Bechard, R. (Eds.). (1996). *The leader of the future.* San Francisco, CA: Jossey-Bass.

Kotler, J.P. (1996). *Leading change.* Boston, MA: Harvard Business School Press.

Levine, S.P., & Crom, M.A. (1993). *The leader in you: How to win friends, influence people and succeed in a changing world.* New York: Dale Carnegie.

O'Toole, J. (1995). *Leading change: Overcoming the ideology of comfort and the tyranny of custom.* San Francisco, CA: Jossey-Bass.

Senge, P.M. (1990). *The fifth discipline.* New York: Currency Doubleday.

Gerald V. Miller, Ph.D., is president of Gerald V. Miller Associates, a management consulting and training firm. He consults with a variety of Fortune 500 companies and public organizations in the areas of leadership development and managing change. He has over twenty years' experience as a specialist in management, organization, and human resource development. He blends organizational and leadership assessment and training with productivity improvement strategies so that his customers see a quantitative and qualitative return on their investment.

Leadership Dimensions Survey Letter to Participants

To the Participant:

The Leadership Dimensions Survey is designed to assess your leadership skills on four dimensions by providing you with feedback about how others view the leadership practices you use.

Attached are five copies of the Leadership Dimensions Survey. Write your name on each as the person who is being evaluated. Distribute copies of the questionnaire to any five people (peers, subordinates, and/or supervisors) whom you believe know you well enough to comment on what you would do (and do not do) as a leader. *Please distribute all five, as this increases the reliability and validity of the results.*

Ask each respondent to complete the questionnaire anonymously and return it to you (or to the facilitator of your leadership training group) *in a sealed envelope.* A sample of a letter you can give to respondents explaining the purpose of the survey is shown below.

Sample Letter to Respondents Completing the Leadership Dimensions Survey

Dear Respondent:

Attached is one copy of the Leadership Dimensions Survey. I would appreciate it if you could fill out the survey about my own behavior as a leader. The purpose of this survey is to assist me in understanding my own behavior and the impact of that behavior on others in a work setting.

Your honest responses will help me to assess my leadership qualities. Please rate each behavior following the instructions at the top of the survey.

Do not write your name on the survey form. It is designed to be completed anonymously. Please return the completed survey in a sealed envelope marked to my attention [or to the facilitator].

Thank you for your time and honest feedback.

Sincerely,

[your name]

LEADERSHIP DIMENSIONS SURVEY

Gerald V. Miller

Person Being Assessed: _____

Instructions: Think of the person who gave this survey to you to complete, named above. To what extent do the following thirty-two statements apply to this person? For each statement, circle the response that best applies, using the following scale.

Strongly Agree = 3   Inclined to Agree = 2   Inclined to Disagree = 1   Strongly Disagree = 0

This person:

1. Can describe the kind of future that he or she would like to create.	3	2	1	0
2. Has behavior that is congruent with his or her leadership philosophy.	3	2	1	0
3. Is aware of new developments in our field.	3	2	1	0
4. Is consistently an ethical and upstanding leader.	3	2	1	0
5. Can give a clear, specific outcome that would result from change.	3	2	1	0
6. Supports projects and changes, both publicly and privately.	3	2	1	0
7. Has experienced what he or she is talking about and knows what he or she is doing.	3	2	1	0
8. Practices principles of self-accountability.	3	2	1	0
9. Appeals to others to join in the vision of the future.	3	2	1	0
10. Is consistent in practicing what he or she preaches.	3	2	1	0
11. Seeks out challenging opportunities that test and stretch the organization's skills and abilities.	3	2	1	0
12. Encourages team members to be interdependent and empowered team members.	3	2	1	0

Strongly Agree = 3   Inclined to Agree = 2   Inclined to Disagree = 1   Strongly Disagree = 0

13. Has clear and specific reasons for initiating change. | 3 | 2 | 1 | 0

13. Has clear and specific reasons for initiating change.	3	2	1	0
14. Monitors projects and change activities with clear goals, plans, and established milestones.	3	2	1	0
15. Is consistently well-prepared for any project or change effort contingency.	3	2	1	0
16. Is sincere when asking for others' suggestions and opinions.	3	2	1	0
17. Clearly communicates a hopeful and inspiring outlook for the future of the organization.	3	2	1	0
18. Reinforces and rewards the efforts of those who carry out projects and change efforts.	3	2	1	0
19. Typically can provide team members with a thorough understanding of any project or change effort.	3	2	1	0
20. Creates an atmosphere of mutual trust during projects and change efforts.	3	2	1	0
21. Understands the resources necessary to put change into effect.	3	2	1	0
22. Experiments and takes risks with new approaches, regardless of the chance of failure.	3	2	1	0
23. Is capable and effective in both technical and leadership abilities.	3	2	1	0
24. Makes a concerted effort to tell the organization about the good work done by the team.	3	2	1	0
25. Shows others how their interests can be realized by joining a common vision.	3	2	1	0
26. Makes personal sacrifices in order to complete projects and to further change efforts.	3	2	1	0
27. Is competent in understanding how all the interacting parts of our organization come together.	3	2	1	0
28. Can always be believed about what he or she is saying.	3	2	1	0

Strongly Agree = 3   Inclined to Agree = 2   Inclined to Disagree = 1   Strongly Disagree = 0

29. Understands the scope of proposed changes and the impact of change on people and the organization.	3	2	1	0
30. Practices innovative leadership that fosters a sense of ownership in others.	3	2	1	0
31. Challenges the status quo regarding the way things are done.	3	2	1	0
32. Typically establishes open, trusting work relationships.	3	2	1	0

Leadership Dimensions Scoring Sheet

Instructions: This scoring sheet is divided into four sections, each representing one dimension of leadership: constancy of purpose, congruity of activity, competency of outcome, or compatibility of values. Transfer the scores given to you by each respondent to the appropriate blanks below. Remember that items are not in numerical order, but are divided by quadrant. Each letter, A through E, represents a different respondent.

    After you have filled in the scores for each question, add them horizontally and divide by the number of responses you received to determine your average score. Write your average scores for each question in the blank provided. Next add the eight average scores for each section and write the number in the blank marked "total."

I. Constancy of Purpose: Profound Strategy and Purposeful Direction

	Respondents					Average
	A	B	C	D	E	
1. Can describe the kind of future that he or she would like to create.	___	___	___	___	___	_____
5. Can give a clear, specific outcome that would result from change.	___	___	___	___	___	_____
9. Appeals to others to join in the vision of the future.	___	___	___	___	___	_____
13. Has clear and specific reasons for initiating change.	___	___	___	___	___	_____
17. Clearly communicates a hopeful and inspiring outlook for the future of the organization.	___	___	___	___	___	_____
21. Understands the resources necessary to put change into effect.	___	___	___	___	___	_____
25. Shows others how their interests can be realized by joining a common vision.	___	___	___	___	___	_____

	Respondents					Average
	A	B	C	D	E	
29. Understands the scope of proposed changes and the impact of change on people and the organization.	___	___	___	___	___	_____

Total _____

II. Congruity of Activity: Profound Strategy and Purposeful Behavior

	Respondents					Average
	A	B	C	D	E	
2. Has behavior that is congruent with his or her leadership philosophy.	___	___	___	___	___	_____
6. Supports projects and changes, both publicly and privately.	___	___	___	___	___	_____
10. Is consistent in practicing what he or she preaches.	___	___	___	___	___	_____
14. Monitors projects and change activities with clear goals, plans, and established milestones.	___	___	___	___	___	_____
18. Reinforces and rewards the efforts of those who carry out projects and change efforts.	___	___	___	___	___	_____
22. Experiments and takes risks with new approaches, regardless of the chance of failure.	___	___	___	___	___	_____
26. Makes personal sacrifices in order to complete projects and to further change efforts.	___	___	___	___	___	_____
30. Practices innovative leadership that fosters a sense of ownership in others.	___	___	___	___	___	_____

Total _____

III. Competency of Outcome: Profound Knowledge and Purposeful Direction

	Respondents					Average
	A	B	C	D	E	
3. Is aware of new developments in our field.	___	___	___	___	___	_____
7. Has experienced what he or she is talking about and knows what he or she is doing.	___	___	___	___	___	_____
11. Seeks out challenging opportunities that test and stretch the organization's skills and abilities.	___	___	___	___	___	_____
15. Is consistently well-prepared for any project or change effort contingency.	___	___	___	___	___	_____
19. Typically can provide team members with a thorough understanding of any project or change effort.	___	___	___	___	___	_____
23. Is capable and effective in both technical and leadership abilities.	___	___	___	___	___	_____
27. Is competent in understanding how all the interacting parts of our organization come together.	___	___	___	___	___	_____
31. Challenges the status quo regarding the way things are done.	___	___	___	___	___	_____

Total _____

IV. Compatibility of Values: Profound Knowledge and Purposeful Behavior

	A	B	C	D	E	Average
	Respondents					
4. Is consistently an ethical and upstanding leader.	___	___	___	___	___	_____
8. Practices principles of self-accountability.	___	___	___	___	___	_____
12. Encourages team members to be interdependent and empowered team members.	___	___	___	___	___	_____
16. Is sincere when asking for others' suggestions and opinions.	___	___	___	___	___	_____
20. Creates an atmosphere of mutual trust during projects and change efforts.	___	___	___	___	___	_____
24. Makes a concerted effort to tell the organization about the good work done by the team.	___	___	___	___	___	_____
28. Can always be believed about what he or she is saying.	___	___	___	___	___	_____
32. Typically establishes open, trusting work relationships.	___	___	___	___	___	_____

Total _____

LEADERSHIP DIMENSIONS MAP

Instructions: Plot your scores for each quadrant. For example, if you received a score of 19 for Quadrant I, Constancy of Purpose, mark the score on both the Profound Strategy and Purposeful Direction lines. Then draw a rule perpendicular to each line and make an X where the two lines meet in the quadrant. Do the same for your scores in each of the other quadrants as shown in the example.

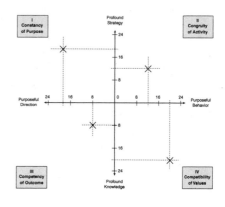

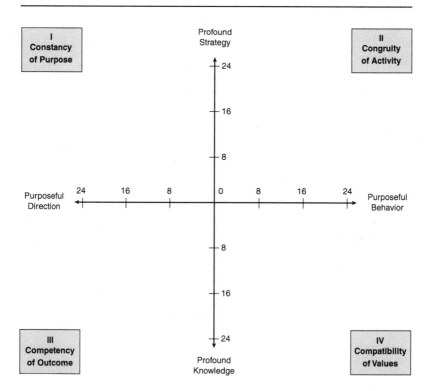

LEADERSHIP DIMENSIONS INTERPRETATION SHEET

Instructions: The most crucial step for learning is to answer the questions, "So what?" and "Now what?" Now that you have completed your Leadership Dimensions Scoring Sheet, you will want to interpret what the scores have to say and take action to improve your leadership skills. Utilizing what you have learned about how you behave in real-world leadership situations, you can make plans for your professional development.

The Leadership Dimensions Survey is interpreted on an item-by-item basis, as well as by comparison of total category scores. You will be able to determine the following information from your scores.

Individual Item Scores

Average scores for *individual items* of 2.0 and above reflect strengths, that is, respondents are telling you that they observe your use of this practice.

Average scores for items of 1.7 to 1.9 are questionable, that is, the total itself provides insufficient information on which to draw a conclusion. You must, instead, look at the spread of scores to determine whether the average score reflects a strength or a weakness. For example, you may receive a score of 1.8 because four people were "inclined to agree" about that item and one person was "inclined to disagree." This would not reflect a weakness. However, if you receive one "strongly agree," one "inclined to agree," and two "inclined to disagree," you may need to improve on that item.

Average scores of 1.6 or lower reflect weaknesses.

Category Scores

For each dimension, look at the total score (sum of all averages). Use the following scale to determine your skill level:

    0 to 9 = Skills Need Significant Improvement
    10 to 19 = Skills Are Adequate, but Could Be Improved
    20 to 24 = Excellent Employment of the Skills

This will help you to apply what you have learned about yourself. For best results, focus on dimensions on which you scored between 10 and 19 (areas for improvement) and between 0 and 9 (areas requiring concerted effort).

Also address individual questions on which your average score was 1.6 or lower, which reflects a weakness, and between 1.7 and 1.9, which reflects a "wait and see" attitude on the part of the respondents.

What can you do to make improvements in each of the quadrants? Read all of the suggestions that follow the interpretation of your scores and then complete the Leadership Dimensions Action Planning Sheet.

Constancy of Purpose

Low (0 to 9) scores in this quadrant indicate that the following areas require improvement:

- Being able to describe the future toward which you are leading your team;
- Formulating clear, specific reasons and outcomes before initiating changes;
- Showing others how their interests can be realized by achieving a common vision and purpose and inspiring them to join you; and
- Showing your understanding of proposed changes and the impact they will have on people and the organization.

Suggestions for Improvement

- Take a course in public speaking or presentation skills.
- Read a book about motivating others and practice what you have learned.
- Develop your interpersonal skills in the areas of opening up and sharing your vision, purpose, and concerns with others.

Congruity of Activity

Low (0 to 9) scores in this quadrant indicate that the following areas require improvement:

- Backing up what you have said, both publicly and privately;
- Monitoring and reinforcing any project or change efforts;
- Fostering a sense of ownership in your team;
- Personally sacrificing to further any project or change; and
- Practicing innovative leadership.

Suggestions for Improvement

- Initiate third-party shadowing, for example, ask a trusted advisor to spend extensive time with you to observe your behavior and provide feedback to you.

- Begin daily "journaling" to note any behaviors that might lead others to believe that you are saying one thing and doing another.

Competency of Outcome

Low (0 to 9) scores in this quadrant indicate that the following areas require improvement:

- Keeping abreast of and ahead of any new developments in your field of expertise;

- Balancing your leadership skills with top-notch technical skills;

- Challenging the status quo and finding new ways of doing work; and

- Rolling up your sleeves and doing the actual work along with your team members.

Suggestions for Improvement

- Obtain just-in-time, experiential training that provides you with actual work skills.

- Request to be mentored by a trusted expert practitioner, someone who has a reputation for excellent application skills.

Compatibility of Values

Low (0 to 9) scores in this quadrant indicate that the following areas require improvement:

- Being responsible and accountable;

- Creating an atmosphere of mutual trust through open and direct communication;

- Communicating your personal and the organization's ethical standards of operation and values; and

- Encouraging team members to be empowered and interdependent.

Suggestions for Improvement

- Attend experiential business ethics training with emphasis on job satisfaction, cooperation, achievement, creativity, tolerance, dignity and respect, truth, honor, and loyalty.

- With the aid of a trusted consultant, conduct a values clarification activity with your team.

LEADERSHIP DIMENSIONS ACTION PLANNING SHEET

Summary

The quadrant in which I scored the lowest was _____.
List the questions on which you scored 1.6 or lower and 1.7 to 1.9 below.
These indicate areas for improvement.

_____

_____

_____

_____

      Statements in the other three quadrants for which I scored 1.6 or
lower include:

_____

_____

_____

_____

_____

Planning

1. As a result of this survey I have learned:

   _____

   _____

   _____

2. The cost of not making changes would be:

   _____

   _____

   _____

3. In order to improve my leadership I must:

   Continue doing: _____

   _____

Start doing: _____

_____

Stop doing: _____

_____

4. My sources for help include:

Mentors: _____

_____

_____

Training: _____

_____

_____

Readings and resources: _____

_____

_____

Other: _____

_____

_____

5. To ensure success I will:

_____

_____

_____

_____

_____

6. I will know I have been successful when:

_____

_____

_____

_____

_____

7. I will improve by taking the following actions:

Action	Start Date	Complete By

Introduction
to the Presentation and Discussion Resources Section

The Presentation and Discussion Resources Section is a collection of articles of use to every facilitator—theories, background, models, and methods to challenge facilitators' thinking, enrich their professional development, and assist their clients (internal and external) with productive change. These articles may be used as a basis for lecturettes, as handouts in training sessions, or as background reading material.

This section will provide you with a variety of useful ideas, theoretical opinions, teachable models, practical strategies, and proven intervention methods. The articles will add richness and depth to your training and consulting knowledge and skills. They will challenge you to think differently, explore new concepts, and experiment with new interventions. The articles will continue to add a fresh perspective to your work.

The 1999 Annual: Volume 1, Training includes ten articles, in the following categories:

Individual Development: Personal Growth
Time Management for Those Who Hate It
by Beverly Robinson and Lisa De Diemar

Individual Development: Change and Risk Taking
Risk Taking for Leaders by Herbert S. Kindler

Communication: Communication Styles, Modes, and Patterns
Leading Training Through Questions by Marlene Caroselli

The Customer Mind Reader: Secrets of Understanding Your
Customer by Peter R. Garber

Communication: Technology
Using the Internet To Identify Training Needs
by Brooke Broadbent

Media Selection Revisited: Training in the Age of Interactive
Technology by Zane L. Berge

Groups and Teams: Group Development
Team Training: Facilitating Real-Time Team Learning
by Emile A. Robert, Jr., and Barbara Pate Glacel

Groups and Teams: Techniques To Use with Groups
Managing Time in Class by Scott B. Parry

Consulting: OD Theory and Practice
The Shift from Training to Performance
by Dana Gaines Robinson and James C. Robinson

Consulting: Consulting Strategies and Techniques
How To Design and Guide Debriefing
by Sivasailam "Thiagi" Thiagarajan

Facilitating: Theories and Models of Facilitating
SEDUCE: An Effective Approach to Experiential Learning
by Lori L. Silverman and Linda Ernst

Facilitating: Evaluating
Making the Transfer Process Work by Paul L. Garavaglia

As with previous *Annuals,* this volume covers a wide variety of topics. The range of articles presented should encourage a good deal of thought-provoking discussion about the present and future of HRD. Other articles on specific subjects can be located by using our comprehensive *Reference Guide to Handbooks and Annuals.* This book, which is updated regularly, indexes the contents of all the *Annuals* and the *Handbooks of Structured Experiences.* With each revision, the *Reference Guide* becomes a complete, up-to-date, and easy-to-use resource for selecting appropriate materials from the *Annuals* and *Handbooks.*

Here and in the *Reference Guide,* we have done our best to categorize the articles for easy reference; however, many of the articles encompass a range of topics, disciplines, and applications. If you do not find what you are looking for under one category, we encourage you to look under a related category. In come cases we may place an article in the "Training" *Annual* that also has implications for "Consulting," and vice versa. As the field of HRD becomes more sophisticated, what is done in a training context is based on the needs of, and affects, the organization. Similarly, from a systemic viewpoint, anything that affects individuals in an organization has repercussions throughout the organization, and vice versa.

It is for this reason that the new "Organization" category has been added to the 1999 volumes. We encourage you not to limit yourself by the categorization system that we have developed, but to explore all the contents of both volumes of the *Annual* in order to realize the full potential for learning and development that each offers.

TIME MANAGEMENT FOR THOSE WHO HATE IT

Beverly Robinson and Lisa De Diemar

Abstract: Effective time management may depend more on personality than on knowledge of time management. One hundred forty individuals, both students and professionals, were given a questionnaire consisting of an abbreviated Personal Style Inventory (PSI) (Hogan & Champagne, 1980), Time-Management Personality Profile (TMPP) (Seid & Piker, 1995), and questions related to self-perceived time-management effectiveness. A positive correlation was found between the judging-perceiving dimension on the *Myers-Briggs Type Indicator* (Briggs & Briggs-Myers, 1977) and time-management effectiveness on the TMPP. The participants with high judging scores on the Myers-Briggs scored significantly higher in time-management competence than did individuals with higher perceiving scores on the Myers-Briggs.

Thus, knowing an individual's PSI scores can help trainers adapt their teaching styles and materials to obtain better results in helping perceivers to achieve better time management. Several techniques for doing this are presented in this article.

$\mathbf{T}$ ime management is big business. From one of the first time-management books (McCay, 1959) to the present, it remains a hot topic. *First Things First* (Covey, Merrill, & Merrill, 1994) was on the *New York Times* and *Business Week* best-seller lists. *The Seven Habits of Highly Effective People* (Covey, 1989) was number twelve on "*USA Today*'s Top 100 Best Sellers for 1996" and continued to be in the top fifty best sellers through September 1997 (*USA Today*, 1997).

A great deal of money has been devoted to the subject by the business industry, computer industry, and large bookstores. Computer hardware and software have been developed to integrate time management into one's personal life and the popular "Dummies" series now has time management on its list of titles.

Recently, time management was ranked nineteenth out of forty-two of the most frequent organizational training topics and was provided by 62 percent of the organizations surveyed (*Training Magazine*, 1997).

Even with all the training available in time management, a recent Internet survey of over 150 business professionals in the United States and Canada indicated that most people waste at least one hour every working day because of disorganization and poor time management (*TrainingNet*, 1996). This conclusion led us to our present study.

PART 1: THE STUDY

Reason for the Study

Effective time management may depend more on personality than on knowledge of time management. Research shows a correlation between the perceiving-judging (P-J) index of the *Myers-Briggs Type Indicator* (MBTI) (Briggs & Briggs-Myers, 1977) and time management (Williams, Verble, Price, & Layne, 1995). For this study we analyzed individual personality preferences on the P-J continuum in respect to individuals' preferences in their approach to time management and their self-perceived time-management effectiveness.

Methodology

One hundred forty questionnaires were completed by males and females from a variety of occupations and educational backgrounds. The individuals were students, engineers, health care workers, and physicians. The questionnaires were completed in three settings: work, the university classroom, or home.

The questionnaire contained forty-four questions, twenty-five of which were Likert-scale; ten used a 0 to 5 forced choice; three were multiple choice; and six were open-ended. Three sections measured time-management personality profile, personal style inventory, and the participants' self-perceived time-management effectiveness.

Methodology: Questionnaire Section 1

Section 1 was based on the Time-Management Personality Profile (TMPP) (Seid & Piker, 1995) and determined the participants' attention to task, type of focus, approach to structure, style of processing, and strategy of action. The questions were arranged so the participants did not know the categories or scoring. One question was taken from each category. See the sample questions and the dimensions in Figures 1 through 5.

As seen in Figure 1, the extremes of the dimension "attention to task" are "divergent" and "convergent." Those having a high score in the attention to task category are considered divergent, and a low score is considered convergent.

Divergent thinking involves expanding a problem and looking at it from all angles and possibilities. A person with divergent thinking will question and request basic facts and opinions, gather as much information as possible, and generate various options for solving a problem. A divergent thinker wants to make sure the problem is thoroughly understood before proceeding. Divergent thinkers expand the problem, thus creating a larger picture (Albrecht, 1980).

Convergent thinkers operate by narrowing the problem to a smaller, more manageable size and perspective. They exclude options in order to focus on those that are left in great detail and analyze them. They reduce until they create a smaller, more detailed picture to act on (Albrecht, 1980).

As shown in Figure 2, the extremes of the dimension "type of focus" are "detailed" and "global." Those having a high score in the type of focus category are considered detailed, and those with a low score are considered global. *Detail-oriented* people focus on facts and specific solutions to an issue or problem. They gather information to support their positions and focus on the here-and-now (Seid & Piker, 1995).

4 = Almost Always 3 = Often 2 = Sometimes 1 = Almost Never		
	Divergent	**Convergent**
	4	1
I have so many "to do" lists that I don't know where to begin.		
I become distracted by the unimportant while I am in the middle of the important.		
My mind wanders when I'm working alone.		
I have scraps of paper scattered about with bits of information on them.		
I put off today what I can do tomorrow.		

Figure 1. Attention to Task: Divergent/Convergent

4 = Almost Always 3 = Often 2 = Sometimes 1 = Almost Never		
	Detailed	**Global**
	4	1
I can make decisions about minor details without needing to know how the overall plan is coming together.		
I am good at mapping out the steps needed to complete a project.		
In the midst of working on a project, attending to minor details as they come up helps me to keep on track.		
I am very precise in how I handle projects.		
I enjoy implementing the details of a project more than I do envisioning the end result.		

Figure 2. Type of Focus: Detailed/Global

4 = Almost Always	3 = Often	2 = Sometimes	1 = Almost Never

	Tight	Loose
	4	1
I know where I have filed most of my important papers.		
I keep my "to-do" list handy.		
I am uncomfortable when my desk is overcrowded with papers.		
I keep track of all of my important deadlines.		
I think that meetings that do not have an agenda are a waste of my time.		

Figure 3. Approach to Structure: Tight/Loose

4 = Almost Always	3 = Often	2 = Sometimes	1 = Almost Never

	Parallel	Serial
	4	1
A busy environment helps me to work more efficiently.		
I tend to take on several tasks at one time.		
While working on one project, ideas about other projects come to my mind.		
I am eager to start a new project before I even finish an existing project.		
When I talk on the phone during a casual conversation, I also engage in other activities (cooking, grooming, cleaning, etc.).		

Figure 4. Style of Processing: Parallel/Serial

4 = Almost Always 3 = Often 2 = Sometimes 1 = Almost Never		
	Reactive	Proactive
	4	1
I put off making decisions until a situation becomes urgent.		
I prepare for things at the last minute.		
I avoid delegating work until it is absolutely necessary.		
I find it difficult to make time for the unexpected.		
I find myself working long hours and never catching up.		

Figure 5. Strategy of Action: Reactive/Proactive

Globally oriented people focus on the possibilities of the future rather than on the facts of the current situation. They envision what might be and gather others' thoughts and do not necessarily deal with details.

The extremes of the dimension "approach to structure" are "tight" and "loose," as seen in Figure 3. A high score in the approach to structure category is considered tight and a low score is considered loose. *Tightly structured* people like to have firm control when accomplishing tasks. They prefer meetings that start on time and have an agenda. *Loosely structured* people prefer flexibility over control when accomplishing tasks. For them, meetings starting late and proceeding without an agenda are all right. Tightly structured people have specific places to put specific information. Loosely structured people put information wherever is convenient at the time, resulting in many scraps of paper with valuable information scattered on their desks (Seid & Piker, 1995).

The extremes of the dimension "style of processing" are "parallel" and "serial," shown in Figure 4. Those having a high score in the style of processing category are considered parallel and those having a low score are considered serial. *Parallel* processors are comfortable performing more than one task at a time; *serial* processors prefer to focus on the task at hand (Seid & Piker, 1995).

Parallel processors often have multiple projects in progress on their desks, at varying levels of completeness. Serial processors usually have one project on their desks and know exactly what needs to be done and how long it will take to complete. They may be involved with multiple projects, but they proceed on a specified course.

The extremes of the dimension "strategy of action" are "reactive" and "proactive," shown in Figure 5. Those having a high score in the strategy of action category are considered reactive and those having a low score are considered proactive. *Reactive* people do not recognize that there is a problem until it is upon them. At that time, they have lost many of their best options for solving it (Albrecht, 1980). These individuals do not plan ahead to avoid problems. Instead they end up putting fires out or trying to meet last-minute deadlines that are self-imposed.

In contrast, *proactive* individuals plan their weekly and daily events based on what they want to accomplish. They make a plan and follow it and do not let circumstances or procrastination get in their way. Consequently, they rarely find themselves in last-minute crisis situations (Seid & Piker, 1995).

Methodology: Questionnaire Section 2

In Section 2, the participants were asked ten forced-answer questions based on the Personal Style Inventory (Hogan & Champagne, 1980) to determine their perceiving-judging (P-J) preference on the *Myers-Briggs Type Indicator* (MBTI). The typology preference was determined by using paired-answer questions. Participants scored the pairs from 0 to 5 (0 meaning negative or no feelings and 5 meaning strong feelings).

A person who scores higher toward the judging (J) dimension tends to choose closure over open options and to establish deadlines and take them seriously. For J's, work comes before everything else. A person scoring high on the perceiving (P) dimension prefers to keep things open and fluid, is more apt to resist making decisions, and tends to look at deadlines as something that can be put off or ignored. For P's, the work does not have to get done before play or rest begins (Keirsey & Bates, 1984).

Methodology: Questionnaire Section 3

In Section 3, the participants were asked a number of questions to determine their thoughts and feelings about time management. This section focused on the individuals' self-perceived time-management effectiveness, specifically looking at their effectiveness with time management, attitude toward time management, and attitude toward learning time management. The questions were based on a 0 to 5 scale.

Results

A statistically significant relationship at more than .05 was found among six of the eight dimensions of the TMPP and the P-J continuum using the SAS System statistical method. Table 1 summarizes the coefficients of the study findings. Relationships were found in the following dimensions: attention to task, approach to structure, strategy of action, effectiveness with time management, attitude toward time management, and ability to learn time management. The following conclusions were drawn:

- *Attention to Task:* J's are more convergent and P's more divergent.

- *Approach to Structure:* J's take a tight approach and P's operate with looser structure.

- *Strategy of Action:* J's tend to act proactively and P's tend to react.

- *Effectiveness:* J's believe they are effective at time management and P's believe they are less effective at time management.

- *Attitude Toward Time Management:* J's have a positive attitude toward time management and P's have a less positive attitude toward time management.

- *Learning Time Management:* J's have a positive attitude toward learning time management and P's have a less positive attitude about learning time management.

The answers to the qualitative questions further supported the results. Figure 6 provides a sample of responses from the participants. Quotes are taken directly from the surveys.

We can see that there are clear differences between J's and P's in their attention to task, approach to structure, strategy of action and attitudes toward time management, that is, J's are better at traditional time management. The question then becomes, "Does it matter?"

Although we believe that J's as well as P's have areas to improve (e.g., flexibility and openness), we are focusing on the P's because the current nature of the workplace most often demands competent time management. Many types of organizations are, by their nature, deadline driven, such as publishing, manufacturing, or technology. Many companies have reduced the size of their work forces to maximize profits. When this occurs, fewer people must complete for the same amount of work, which creates the necessity for people to meet deadlines and produce under increased pressure (Noer, 1993). Furthermore, people are being called on and expected to excel at juggling both personal and professional priorities (Connor, 1997).

Type	Task	Focus	Structure	Process	Action	Effect	Attitude	Learning
Perceiving								
Coefficient	0.21926	0.08790	0.29821	0.06320	0.24081	0.21381	0.38127	0.17964
Significance	0.0109	0.3107	0.0004	0.4665	0.0049	0.0121	0.0001	0.0371
Number	134	135	136	135	135	136	136	135
Judging								
Coefficient	0.21068	0.09647	0.030542	0.05529	0.25677	0.21189	0.38316	0.14403
Significance	0.0149	0.2675	0.0003	0.5257	0.0027	0.0133	0.0001	0.0968
Number	133	134	135	134	134	136	135	134

Table 1. Coefficients of Findings

Attention to Task:	
Convergent J's	**Divergent P's**
"I wanted to be in control of my life by being organized."	"I'm not the most organized person in the world. Usually, it tends to complicate my life and spawn chaos."
"I want a step-by-step plan."	"Sometimes I like to plan things out, yet other times I enjoy being spontaneous. I think time management may reduce my stress and make me more organized, and I would use my time more appropriately."
Approach to Structure:	
Tight J's	**Loose P's**
"I enjoy having my ducks in a row."	"I've been unconventional. For example, I almost always watch TV or do something while I'm studying."
"I like the military precision approach to ensure that all possible variances are reasonably accounted for and the proper preparations are made to ensure everything is completed. When things go as planned, it leaves me free to pursue other tasks. When unexpected problems occur, they are easier to deal with."	"I couldn't stand to write everything down and schedule every minute of my day. The small exposure I've had to time management training has been devoted to activities I know I'd never do."
Strategy for Action:	
Proactive J's	**Reactive P's**
"[I like to be] able to use the resource called 'time' in a manner that accomplishes my short-term and long-term goals and commitments."	"I know that my procrastination will catch up to me one day in my career, and I need to learn some skills that will help change the way I use my time."
"I learned how important it is to effectively budget my time so that I'm able to stay on task and meet deadlines without headaches!!"	"I like the way that I'm lazy and will get to it when I can."

Figure 6. Sample Responses to Qualitative Questions

Attitudes Toward Time Management and Learning About It:	
J's	**P's**
"Always looking for ways to improve. Always looking for ways to be even more efficient."	"[Time management] is not a priority with me."
"I'm pretty organized now, but I love learning tricks to develop my skills more."	"Why is [time management] so important to everyone? Why can't they also help motivate exceptional procrastinators?"

Figure 6. Sample Responses to Qualitative Questions *(continued)*

What Next?

The correlation between an individual's personality and his or her attitude toward time management was determined. We next tried to determine what the findings could mean for people who want to use time management, yet are having difficulty incorporating it into their daily lives. We attempted to find ways to help them to use the tools of time management.

PART 2: IMPLICATIONS FOR TRAINING

Suggestions for P's

Trainers can help P's become more convergent, tight, and proactive so that they can, if they so choose, better cope with job demands and pressures and meet employers' expectations.

The following tools and techniques are best if they can become part of whatever routine an individual has, with only a slight adjustment in the person's routine or ritual. For example, if the person gets coffee or turns on the computer at a certain time each day, help him or her link an organizing task to that activity until it is habitual.

Attention to Task

Problem: Divergent people can sometimes be identified by piles on their desks and the fact that they do not know where to locate items.

Solution 1: Use a simple sorting system. Sorting could be done while standing up or talking on the telephone (not recommended when listening carefully or empathetically is necessary!) so that the divergent person would feel a sense of physical movement. Items could be sorted into categories such as:

- *File:* Information that must be accessed in the future, such as an article to use for a presentation. If someone else will have a copy or it is on disk, it can be thrown away.

- *Read:* Information that must be read, such as reports and professional publications. Do a reality check by asking, "Am I really going to need this?" and then place the material in a reading pile or in the trash. (A helpful tactic for minimizing stacks of periodicals is to tear out the articles desired after a quick review of the table of contents.)

- *Refer:* Information that others need or could act on if properly delegated, such as answering a letter or returning a call. Using Post-it™ Notes or writing instructions directly on the document saves time. On a trip to the rest room or coffee machine, take the items and put them in appropriate mailboxes or hand them to people.

- *Trash:* Throw away information that is not useful immediately.

- *Act:* Information that requires action. If it can be acted on immediately, do it right away. Do not handle material more than once! For immediate action (that day) leave the item on the desk. For deferred action, such as preparation for an upcoming meeting, use a tickler file. Entering an activity in a planner is a plus, but it is unlikely behavior for a P.

Solution 2: It may be possible to convince some P's that a desk filing system would work, such as a tickler file, one with thirty-one days for the current month and eleven other months. Work can then be placed in the day or month it is to be completed. At the end of the month, the next month is separated into the thirty-one slots.

Solution 3: Because divergent people draw energy from variety and what seems interesting at the moment, a master list of tasks to be accomplished, from which they can choose one they would like to work on for a period of time and others that they can tackle when they reach roadblocks or are bored, may be helpful. A master list helps them to keep everything that needs to be done in one place. The master list could be kept in various formats:

- A legal pad kept on the desk or carried in a briefcase;
- A hot list half-page insert in a planner that could be moved from one day to the next;
- A sheet behind a tab in a regular planner; or
- A page marker inserted in a plastic divider sleeve that can be moved from day to day.

In any case, items would have to be copied to a new page occasionally. A master list can also be placed on the computer and maintained daily. Completed items can be deleted from the list simply.

Solution 4: Give the P's a "desk survey" every six months, asking them about items on their desks:

- *Is it functional?* Most items on the desk should serve a purpose, for example, a container for paper clips, standing files for "in" and "out," pending material, and a computer.
- *Do I like it?* If it is not functional, it should have personal value and give pleasure, such as family pictures, miniature car replicas, or stone paperweights.
- *Is this the best place for it?* If a computer consumes a great deal of desk space, it could be moved. Although pictures and memorabilia bring pleasure, they clutter a desktop and hanging or placing them on a non-work surface could be more functional.

Solution 5: Suggest various organizing tools for the desk: stacked trays (hold in/out boxes, pending, current work), pencil container (holds pens, pencils, or highlighters and may have room for paper clips, rubber bands, and scissors), stationery caddie (holds letterhead, envelopes, stamps), address file (holds addresses or phone numbers or business cards alphabetically), Post-it™ caddie (holds one or more sizes of Post-it™ Notes), work station organizers (holds computer, keyboard, printer, disks, and compact disks), vertical rack (holds files horizontally), etc. Organizing tools for the office can also be suggested: bulletin board (cork or self-stick boards), wall pocket (holds material and can be sorted), shelf (holds books, periodicals, binders, or personal items), yearly calendar (can be written on with marker or pen), drawing boards (chalk or white board), etc.

Approach to Structure

Problem 1: Loosely structured people leave scraps of paper with valuable information lying around because they put them where it is convenient at the time.

Solution: Post-it™ Notes can be used and applied in the proper place so that information does not get lost. A large bulletin board with category columns (calls, meetings, deadlines, etc.) that could be used to post notes would meet the P's need to not waste time recording something and yet still keep it in an organized fashion. Labeled files can also be placed in a handy place such as a drawer or flip-top file so that notes can be immediately put in the proper category. Notes can also be affixed in a planner on the day they must be addressed.

Problem 2: Loosely structured people begin with a project system, but tend to alter or abandon it as the project progresses, often because they prefer flexibility over control. If they are also divergent, they may do this because they continue to question the system or gather more information to find the best approach.

Solution: Because the system exists in the beginning, it can be placed on a white board or a wall calendar used only for the project, or the check points of the project can be placed in a planner. Because the system is visible, it may assist in keeping P's on track. P's can also ask for help from another person to remind them to keep using the system until it becomes a habit, if that is critical to completing the project. The "helper" would hold the individual accountable for achieving checkpoints. Even if P's change their approach, having checkpoints will move them toward the deadline.

Strategy of Action

Problem: Reactive P's tend to put off today what they think they can do tomorrow, which results in their spending time reacting to deadlines and crises.

Solution 1: P's often tend to postpone things because they are easily distracted or interrupted. To prevent this, they can arrange their offices so that they face away from the door, close their doors, or put "do not disturb" signs on their doors. If an organization offers flex-time, P's can come in early or stay late so that for part of their work day there will be fewer distractions.

Solution 2: Set up mini goals by breaking projects down in steps to meet deadlines on time. Place the mini goals on a calendar or planner. If necessary, have them create false deadlines or dates by which the project should be done ahead of the date it *must* be accomplished to fool themselves into sticking to the task. Since P's often think that tasks can be completed more quickly than is realistic or that the task is easier than it actually is, have them make an estimate of how long each part of the task will take and then add 15 percent, adjusting the timing of their mini deadlines accordingly. To complete a proposal needed in three weeks, the deadline should be in eighteen days.

Solution 3: P's can try the 5-minute plan. Have them think to themselves, "I'm going to work on this item from my to-do list for 5 minutes without doing anything else!" Plan several 5-minute segments throughout the day. An alarm clock, alarm watch, or computerized reminder can be set to become aware of how time gets away from them. Alarm clocks can also be used to remind P's to return to a task or to apply the 5-minute plan.

Attitude Toward Time Management and Learning Time Management

We know from the P's attitudes toward time management shown in Figure 6 that simply teaching time-management techniques, even when linking them to a routine (or lack of it), may not take hold.

This is not a problem unless it jeopardizes someone's job in some way. However, although their jobs may not be at stake, P's would probably accomplish more and have better working relationships if they improved their time management. If providing tools for their use is not successful, the next level is to change their attitudes or motivation. Some possible ways to motivate P's or change their attitudes are listed below:

1. Find out about the person's stress level. Show him or her how time management could reduce some of the stress. For example, if the person has to work late continually to catch up (and dislikes that) show him or her how planning can reduce the last-minute rush by reviewing how a just-completed task could have been done with less pressure.

2. Because multiple options are usually important to P's, impress on them that lack of time management reduces their options for other important matters. For example, being engaged in a last-minute rush to meet a deadline reduces the amount of time available for experimenting with various new ideas.

3. If they believe they do exceptional work and seek to excel, show them how this can be brought about through time management. For example, show them that with planning they would have more time to brainstorm, do research, refine writing, or solicit feedback.

4. Diffuse concerns about time management being rigid and taking too much time by showing P's how to plan their spontaneous time by entering it in their planner or by planning a longer time than a task will take so that there is extra time upon completion. Show them how much time can be gained by planning.

If these suggestions do not work, it may help to approach P's from the point of view of integrity and trustworthiness. Most people want to be seen as having integrity, "the quality or state of being of sound moral principles; uprightness, honesty, and sincerity" (Guralnik, 1970), and as being trustworthy, dependable, and reliable (Guralnik, 1970). Putting the two together means that people do what they say they will do. If people can be shown that their integrity and/or trustworthiness is at stake when they manage their time badly, it may provide the motivation necessary to make beneficial changes. *First Things First* (Covey, Merrill, & Merrill, 1994) addresses both qualities. Using integrity and establishing trustworthiness are within Covey's context of the principle-centered life and Quadrant II time management (spending time on what is important but not yet urgent, which focuses on long-term and relational results). The following suggestions for exercising integrity at the moment of choice may be helpful to P's.

1. Work to translate your principles into the decision moments for each day.

2. Use a specific question in moments of choice and review it often throughout the day, for example, "Am I living by my principles if I make this choice?"

3. At the start of each day and as you make each decision, think about the promises and commitments you have made and whether you are keeping them.

4. Remain aware of how you usually respond in moments of choice, such as answering, thinking, choosing desirable over necessary actions, or delaying decisions.

5. At important decision points, stop and analyze factors that affect you, such as urgency, others' expectations, history, wants and desires, etc.

6. Evaluate the long-term consequences of each choice. Did the choice benefit your long-term goals? Did it help you build relationships with significant people?

If these suggestions fail, it may be necessary for the P to find another position, another organization, or another career where meeting deadlines is not a critical indicator of job success.

Summary

Studies of personal styles and time-management styles reveal correlations that can help trainers to improve the time-management abilities of certain types of personalities. "Judgers" tend to be more focused and have better time-management habits and attitudes. "Perceivers" tend to be more unfocused and have less effective time-management habits and less positive attitudes toward time management. Certain techniques can be used by trainers to help perceivers approach time management from their own perspectives and apply principles of time management that better suit their personal style.

References

Albrecht, K. (1980). *Brain power*. Englewood Cliffs, NJ: Prentice Hall.

Briggs, K., & Briggs-Myers, I. (1977). *Myers-Briggs type indicator*. Palo Alto, CA: Consulting Psychologists Press.

Connor, L. Personal communication, September 24, 1997.

Covey, S.R. (1989). *The seven habits of highly effective people*. New York: Simon & Schuster.

Covey, S.R., Merrill, A.R., & Merrill, R.R. (1994). *First things first*. New York: Simon & Schuster.

Hogan, R.C., & Champagne, D.W. (1980). *Personal style inventory*. In J.W. Pfeiffer & J.E. Jones (Eds.) *The 1980 annual handbook for group facilitators*. San Francisco: Jossey-Bass/Pfeiffer.

Keirsey, D., & Bates, M. (1984). *Please understand me* (5th ed.). Del Mar, CA: Prometheus Menesis.

Lakein, A. (1973). *How to get control of your time and your life*. New York: P.H. Wyden.

Mayer, J.J. (1995). *Time management for dummies*. Foster City, CA: IDG Books.

McCay, J.T. (1959). *The management of time*. Englewood Cliffs, NJ: Prentice Hall.

Noer, D.M. (1993). *Healing the wounds: Overcoming the trauma of layoffs and revitalizing downsized organizations*. San Francisco, CA: Jossey-Bass.

Seid, D., & Piker, K. (1995). Time-management personality profile. In J.W. Pfeiffer (Ed.), *The 1995 Annual: Volume 2, Consulting*. San Francisco: Jossey-Bass/Pfeiffer.

Training Magazine. (1997, October). Industry report, *Training Magazine, 34*, 55.

Training Magazine. (1997, October). Training today: Franklin Quest and Covey to merge, *Training Magazine, 34*, 14–15.

TrainingNet. (1996, December). *TrainingNet survey confirms poor organizational and time management practices damage productivity, morale.* http://www.trainingnet.com/magazine/get_organized.htime management.

USA Today. (1997, September 25). *USA Today's* 150 best-selling books in the country. http://www.usatoday.com/life/enter/books/leb1.htime management.

Williams, R.L., Verble, J.S., Price, D.E., Layne, B.H. (1995). Relationship between time-management practices and personality indices and types. *Journal of Psychological Type, 34,* 36–42.

Beverly Robinson, Ph.D., *is a full professor of communication at Wright State University, Dayton, Ohio, where she directs the basic interpersonal communication course. Her consulting business, the Communication Connection, provides training and consulting to area businesses. She has written numerous books and articles on interpersonal communication, teams, and training topics.*

Lisa De Diemar *is the program administrator for the Internal Medicine and Transitional Year Residency at Kettering Medical Center, Kettering, Ohio. She coordinates the residency programs, develops procedure and protocols, develops material advertising for the programs, and works with physicians to develop presentations. She graduated from Wright State University, Dayton, Ohio, having earned a Bachelor of Arts degree in organizational communication.*

Risk Taking for Leaders

Herbert S. Kindler

Abstract: Appropriate risk taking is espoused by virtually all organizations, yet little real guidance is offered by or to leaders. This article defines risk as "making a choice to gain a desired outcome under conditions of uncertainty with the possibility of losing something you value." To take appropriate risks, therefore, one must: (1) identify means for improving the odds and the magnitude of potential gains; (2) identify means for reducing exposure to loss; and (3) reduce uncertainty. Additionally, to filter bias, it is important to recognize the degree to which the leader and other stakeholders have a tendency to seek or avoid risks. Suggestions for improving risk-taking performance are presented.

T his article can be used as part of a presentation on improving risk taking in organizations. The material is helpful in workshops and seminars on risk taking, problem solving, decision making, and managing change.

Most organizations espouse the positive aspects of risk taking and honor corporate heroes who have triumphed over daunting odds. Yet, helpful support is often missing. Many organizations state that they "encourage innovation and risk taking," but too often the unspoken tag line is "but don't screw up."

Risk-taking performance can be improved with guidance that helps leaders:

1. To recognize their own tendencies toward risk preference, risk avoidance, or risk neutrality.
2. To deal with potential gain, vulnerability to loss, and uncertainty in ways that support constructive change.

This article presents ways to assess one's own approach to risk taking in order to recognize risks that are worth taking and to adjust risks that are unacceptable in their present form. It also suggests that the inevitable, occasional failure be a source, not of blame, but of learning.

RISK-TAKING TENDENCIES

Individuals fall somewhere along a continuum between risk preference and risk avoidance. Figure 1 describes each orientation. Determine your own orientation toward risk on the continuum in Figure 2.

It is important to know what orientation you bring to each risky situation. People who have risk-avoidance patterns may miss opportunities to influence hoped-for outcomes, while those who have risk-preference patterns may leave themselves, their organizations, and others unnecessarily vulnerable. Risk neutrality reflects a willingness to make either a risky or a conservative choice, based on relevant evidence, rather than on a predisposition.

People with a risk-preference pattern tend to	People with a risk-avoidance pattern tend to
• Underrate uncertainties	• Overrate uncertainties
• Be overly optimistic	• Be overly pessimistic
• Seek excitement and novelty	• Prefer security and comfort
• Overrate or exaggerate the probability of realizing desired outcomes	• Underrate or ignore the probability of realizing desired outcomes
• Decide impulsively *Motto:* Nothing ventured, nothing gained.	• Postpone decisions or close the door of opportunity too quickly *Motto*: Better safe than sorry.

Figure 1. Risk Preference vs. Risk Avoidance

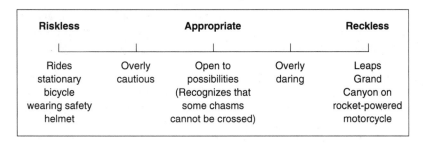

Figure 2. Risk-Taking Continuum

IMPROVING YOUR ODDS OF REALIZING POTENTIAL GAINS

The following sections contain some ways to increase the odds that you will benefit from taking risks.

Clarify Objectives

Prudent risk taking starts with a clear vision of what you value and desire. For example, a risk may be taken in order to improve a process, save time, obtain personal recognition, improve a group's performance ratings, and so on. It is important to know whether your goal is personal, group specific, or organizational and to know whether you are attempting to impress someone, improve a physical process, improve morale, motivate people, or achieve some other result. Often, we focus on one objective and fail to see other likely results. It often is wise to consider the values and desires (objectives) of those who may be affected by our actions or the outcomes. For example, if you are considering taking the risk of instituting a new procedure, you might want to consider the input on those whom this action would affect (the persons who have to implement the procedure, that is, the internal customers of the procedure's output). When you are considering a risk that involves others, some key questions to ask follow:

- What outcomes are needed and wanted? By you? By others involved?
- What other outcomes might result from the proposed action?

For example, a manager may suggest instituting an organizational awards banquet in order to recognize outstanding performers. In order to have a quick "solution" to the problem of how to recognize outstanding performance (to avoid putting any more of their own time into it or to avoid being responsible for the suggestion or the outcome), other managers may agree with the suggestion without exploring its implications or other options. This is an example of risk avoidance. It allows the awards banquet to be seen as the objective, rather than establishing that the objective is rewarding excellent performance and opening up the discussion to other ways in which this could be achieved. It also fails to consider the down sides of an awards banquet (cost, time involved in preparation, the setting up of a competitive environment among employees, the reactions of those employees who are not honored, and so on).

Identify and Evaluate Alternatives

To identify alternative paths to desired outcomes:

- Do not converge too quickly on an action plan. Instead of fishing with a pole, throw out a large net to catch a more varied assortment of possibilities.
- See limitations, obstacles, and restrictions as gifts—as stimuli to challenge your ingenuity and activate your creative juices.
- Rather than choosing between objectionable alternatives, discover or invent other possibilities.

- Do not accept either/or alternatives without first considering the possibility that a different course of action is feasible.

For example, a start-up company's marketing manager proposed that the limited promotional budget be used either for print or for television advertising. Deeper consideration might reveal additional options, such as reaching key customers more effectively and less expensively by means of the Internet or interactive seminars.

To evaluate other possible paths to desired outcomes:

- Recognize that important assessments often cannot be based on quantitative data. Some measures are qualitative—especially when you are measuring what really matters. How else can we assign value to human life, effort, or aesthetics?

Identify Limiting Assumptions

Creative options are springboards to better odds and greater gains. Limiting assumptions such as, "That's not how we do things around here" get in the way of innovative ideas.

In the earlier example of initiating an awards banquet, if the assumption were made that the central task is to create the best possible event, other possibilities will be lost, such as: (1) granting time off to promising first-line supervisors for visits to academic and industry leaders; (2) naming outstanding performers as corporate fellows for a year to tackle projects of their own choosing; (3) inviting employees to lunch with the executive so they can present their ideas.

Choose Action Others Can Support

Identify aspects that would make your decision acceptable to people whose support you need. Evaluate how congruent your action plan is with the goals, values, and priorities of others on whom its success depends. Then ensure that your actions and decisions support their priorities. For example, recognizing individual performance is not appropriate or motivating at a time when teamwork is desired. The payoff is greater—and the support of others in the organization is more likely to be gained—if outstanding team performance is recognized.

REDUCING EXPOSURE TO LOSS

Three strategies reduce the impact of risky decisions that could result in a loss: share the risk with others, limit the possible loss, and diversify.

Share the Risk

Leaders of the past often made bold, unilateral decisions. Now we know that involving others in candid dialogue allows individuals and groups to find fresh ways to align with larger objectives and values—to share the risk.

Risks can be shared in a number of ways. One way is through cooperative relationships, such as partnerships, alliances, or joint ventures. Another common method for distributing risk is through insurance. Each policy holder pays a relatively small price so that none suffers a devastating loss. Bonding is a form of insurance for employees who have access to company money.

For example, an increasingly important risk arena is international trade. In currency swap agreements, the overseas banks guarantee, for a fee, future convertibility of foreign currency at a fixed exchange rate.

Limit the Loss

Limitations prevent tolerable risks from reaching unacceptable levels. Several tactics are available to limit losses, including the following:

- Stop-loss orders to sell (anything traded in an active market) at a specific price.
- Safety nets (a severance package and job-hunting assistance) for people who accept employment on high-risk projects.
- Buffers, such as flex factors in bridges, spare tires, and inventories stored against unanticipated demand.
- Surveillance methods that limit risk, such as security systems, screening of applicants, and conducting unscheduled audits.
- Pilot experiments, trial runs, market tests, and gradual phase-in of new operations.

The most common form of loss limitation is learning from one's own and others' mistakes. The knowledge gained from previous failure is often critical to achieving subsequent success.

Diversify

Portfolio diversification is a time-honored means of preventing major investment losses, especially in volatile markets. Diversification makes sense even for a retailer on a sunny tourist island where the big seller is suntan lotion. The manager might well prepare for rainy days by stocking some umbrellas.

However, as with most loss-reduction tactics, diversification does not always work. In the 1970s, many conglomerates were created that had such poor performance records that Peters and Waterman (1982), in their best-selling book, *In Search of Excellence,* warned executives to limit their focus to core competencies and to "stick to the knitting."

In the earlier example of motivating outstanding performance, instead of a single initiative, leaders could have considered a variety of approaches, such as a formal event, informal lunches, spontaneous money awards, sabbaticals, and intrapreneurship programs that supported innovative employees in creating enterprises within the corporate framework.

REDUCING UNCERTAINTY

Three strategies to reduce uncertainty are described below: gathering information, letting events unfold, and influencing the outcome.

Gathering Information

Before gathering information, it is a good idea to weigh three factors: time, cost, and reliability.

Time

If you take the time to gather and assimilate more data, will a future opportunity really be lost by the delay? Will a delay actually give competitors a significant or even irreversible advantage? Resist deadlines requested by colleagues who are obsessed with quick action. Perhaps a deadline can be extended; a prospective employer may be willing to wait a day or two while you mull over a job decision; or a customer may have exaggerated a need in order to assure delivery before a critical date.

Cost

Is the expense of acquiring more information likely to be recovered by making a better decision? This is the implicit question in poker, when you risk your ante to gain information by "buying" more cards.

Reliability

How reliable is the information you have collected? How valid and dependable are forecasts made by specialists and consultants? When you are deciding whether to buy a mutual fund or whether to undergo heart surgery, you certainly will want to solicit multiple independent opinions.

Letting Events Unfold

If timing is not critical, simply observe events relevant to the risk you are contemplating until the appropriate course of action becomes clear. Even a modest delay may be useful to avoid overly zealous advocacy or heated opposition to win over more deliberate reflection.

Influencing the Outcome

As you review the available information, if the risk is not acceptable, determine how you could intervene to improve the odds of realizing your goals or limiting potential losses. Explore which risk factors can be controlled in ways that are feasible, cost-effective, and ethical.

Do not expect to eliminate all risk. Attempts at total control are usually self-defeating. For example, when the Hunt brothers of Dallas tried to control the price of silver by cornering bullion, they ended up losing over $1 billion in the 1980 silver market crash.

Attempting to influence outcomes too much can backfire. In some cases, exerting less control can have a more positive influence on the outcome. For example, in an era when command-and-control leadership is passé, if managers attempt too much control over the behavior of direct reports, the employees are likely to become overly dependent or resentful. The analysis in Figure 3 can be used to assess the risk inherent in a specific situation.

Situation
Briefly describe a situation you expect to face in which the decision appears risky.

Gains
What outcomes would yield the gains that you desire?
What about this outcome would you value?
How good are the chances that these gains will materialize?
What factors are critical to a successful outcome?
What other options are possibilities?

Losses
What losses might be experienced?
How likely is a negative outcome?
What impact might such losses have on you and other stakeholders?
What is the worst-case scenario?
What would be your recovery or loss-limiting plan?
Is there a way to share the risks?
Can you test your assumptions on a small scale?

Uncertainty
What important uncertainties exist?
Can you obtain more information? If so, at what cost?
Can you reduce uncertainty by waiting for events to unfold? If so, at what cost?
Can you intervene to reduce uncertainty? If so, at what cost?

Action Plan
Considering this situation and your own risk-taking tendency, what specific action steps will you take?

Figure 3. Risk-Taking Analysis

LEARNING FROM RISK

Because taking risks is making a choice to gain a desired outcome under conditions of uncertainty with the possibility of losing something you value, at its core, risk is a measure of ignorance. Therefore, we can improve our future ability to take risks by learning from each experience and by creating risk-friendly environments.

References and Readings

Kindler, H.S. (1997). *Risk taking inventory.* Pacific Palisades, CA: Center for Management Effectiveness.

Kindler, H.S. (1990). *Risk taking: A guide for decision makers* (rev. ed.). Menlo Park, CA: Crisp.

Peters, T.J., & Waterman, R.H. (1982). *In search of excellence.* New York: Harper & Row.

Herbert S. Kindler, Ph.D., is a former industry CEO and professor of management. He graduated from M.I.T. and received his doctorate from UCLA. He has five books in print in nine languages, including Risk Taking *(Crisp). Dr. Kindler has presented hundreds of workshops on risk taking and change, stress management, and managing disagreement and conflict constructively.*

Leading Training Through Questions

Marlene Caroselli

Abstract: As Peter Drucker says, "Leaders know how to ask questions—the right questions." The properly phrased question can help set a course of action, strengthen teams, validate purpose, and help both individuals and organizations avoid costly mistakes. For the trainer committed to intensifying the learning experience and optimizing the retention of what was learned, questions are the perfect tool. The range of questions extends from the simple to the complex; their uses are multi-functional; and their effects demonstrate and develop leadership on many levels.

This paper explores various views of the questioning process, identifies ways to make the environment more response-receptive, suggests questions suitable for various aspects of training, and explores several different types of questions. Although the trainer learns a new skill, the ultimate beneficiary of these ideas and activities is, of course, the participant attending training sessions. This article is filled with suggestions to trainers for using questions more creatively, no matter what the subject matter.

EXTRICATING EXCELLENCE

Ask the typical adult, "How do you get to heaven?" and the answers will be strikingly similar: "You do good deeds," "You lead a virtuous life," or "You live by the Ten Commandments." Ask the typical child, though, and you'll receive answers that diverge instead of converge: "You have to take the God elevator," "You need God magic for that," "When all the bad has been spanked out of you, then you're ready for heaven," or "You go to hell and take a left."

Had the questions been framed differently, would the adult answers have been more creative? I believe they would. Unfortunately, in these turbulent times we ask and answer questions quickly. Consequently, we as trainers often fail to frame questions in a way that will elicit the reactions we hope to receive.

The more attention that is paid to asking questions, the more likely we as trainers are to extricate excellence—in terms of analysis, creativity, and motivation. Read the many views about questions in Figure 1. Which of these most appeals to you? What does this tell you about your own style of questioning?

Here is one technique that can be used in your session to stimulate thoughtful responses to questions. Collect a number of quotations from leading authorities on the topic of the session you are presenting. Print them in large type, one per page, and hang them around the training room. Periodically, call on individuals to select one they especially like and read it aloud for the group. Ask them what relevance the quotation has for them or for the subject matter under consideration.

MAKING THE ENVIRONMENT RESPONSE-RECEPTIVE

Effective trainers view questions as tools: to guide discussion, to quicken the pace of instructional progress, and to encourage in-depth analysis of issues.

Questions for these purposes can be generated by either the trainer or the learners. In order for questions to be learner-generated, a trainer must create the right climate. Effective trainers from the start will offer assurances to the participants, saying, for example, "I like to ask questions. It heightens the tension in the room [Pause for inevitable laughter] and tension is actually a good thing, in moderation. If I call on you and you don't have the an-

Benjamin Disraeli*: "Ignorance never settles a question."

George Edward Moore*: "It appears to me that in ethics, as in all other philosophical studies, the difficulties and disagreements, of which history is full, are mainly due to a very simple cause: namely to the attempt to answer questions without first discovering precisely what question you desire to answer."

Protagoras*: "There are two sides to every question."

Publilius Syrus*: "It is not every question that deserves an answer."

Ella Wheeler Wilcox*: "No question is ever settled until it is settled right."

Alfred North Whitehead**: "The 'silly' question is the first intimation of some totally new development."

Joan Baez***: "Hypothetical questions get hypothetical answers."

Katherine Graham***: "Bromidic though it may sound, some questions don't have answers, which is a terribly difficult lesson to learn."

Ingrid Bengis***: "The real questions refuse to be placated. They barge into your life at the times when it seems most important for them to stay away."

*As quoted in *Familiar Quotations,* John Bartlett, 15th and 125th Anniversary Edition, Emily Morison Beck (Ed.). Boston: Little Brown, 1980.
**As quoted in *Webster's New World Dictionary of Quotable Definitions* (2nd ed.), Eugene E. Brussell (Ed.). Englewood Cliffs, NJ: Prentice Hall, 1988.
***As quoted in *The Quotable Woman: An Encyclopedia of Useful Quotations,* Volume Two, Elaine Partnow (Ed.). Los Angeles: Pinnacle, 1985.

Figure 1. Views on Questions

swer—or maybe you have the answer but you don't want to give it to me— just look me in the eye and say, 'Pick on somebody else, lady.' And I will. It's no problem. Just say or indicate 'Pass,' and I'll move right along."

The instructor can also encourage questions by making a statement such as this: "You'll find me highly interruptible. Please, if something occurs to you, just raise your hand. Don't wait until I finish to ask a question. Let me hear from you whenever there's something that calls for clarification or something you wish to contribute."

The Delphi Technique also can be used to elicit questions that show the depth (or lack of depth) of participants' understanding of the subject matter. Within the first half-hour of the start of class, distribute 3" x 5" index cards while acknowledging that participants are often reluctant to ask questions. Explain that they can write questions on the cards anonymously that they might hesitate to ask publicly. Collect the questions at various times throughout the day and spend a few minutes answering them.

The trainer can also appoint the most gregarious person in the room as the "Question Meister," giving this individual responsibility for keeping his or her finger on the collective pulse of the group and asking questions on their behalf. Participants can forward questions to the Meister throughout the day, and he or she can select the most interesting or appropriate of these to be addressed. Or the Meister could be allowed five minutes every few hours to circulate among the participants and learn what issues they most want clarity on.

Another possibility, if the room is arranged by table groups, is to ask groups periodically to come up with one question each. Typically, if a generic question is put before the group such as, "Are there any questions?" no questions will be asked. To avoid the danger of assuming that silence means understanding, ask groups to formulate at least one question each. Some of the best questions are created during these "required" activities.

Finally, if it is possible to have an outside lecturer address the group later in the day or later in the course, ask groups for lists of ten questions they'd like to ask the expert and to indicate which two on their lists are their "burning" questions.

Questions for Instructional Segments

Waiting until the conclusion of a seminar to review the material through questions is not as effective as short, periodic reviews at the end of each instructional unit. Ask for a volunteer to identify the highlights or call on each group to present a review. To encourage creativity or energize participants, ask teams to prepare a four-word rhyme that summarizes the segment, similar to Bruce Tuckman's (Tuckman & Jensen, 1977) synopsis of team functioning: Form-Storm-Norm-Perform.

Most training sessions have segments for introductions, knowledge transfer, closure, and so on. Each element can be more beneficial for the learner and more satisfying for the trainer with the use of well-thought-out questions. You will want to build your personal collection of questions for each segment. The following are some suggested questions:

Introductions

- What do you hope to take away from this workshop?
- What does your supervisor hope you'll take away?
- What type of learner are you?
- Why are you here today?
- How would you define "leadership"? [Substitute whatever word reflects the course content.]
- What would you like the others at your table to know about you?
- What knowledge has been most valuable to you thus far in your career?

Objectives

- What additional objectives do you think should be part of this class?
- On a scale of 1 (low) to 5 (high), how much do you already know about each objective?
- Which objective on the list surprises you?
- Which objective are you hoping we will spend the least time on?
- How do the listed objectives parallel your own objectives for taking the class?
- Assuming the objectives are met, how will you use your new knowledge when you return to work?
- Which objective represents your top learning priority? In what way?

Discussion of Subject Matter

- What is the most important thing you have learned so far in the session?
- How does the information we have recently covered relate to your work?
- If you were to share what you have learned with a co-worker, what would you highlight?
- What applications does this information have for you as you perform your job?
- What relevance do these issues have to what is happening in the world outside your organization?
- Can you think of a quotation related to what we have just covered?

- What questions might internal or external customers have regarding what we've just learned?
- What comments would you like to make about this instructional module?
- If you were to "teach" someone else what you have just learned, how would you present it?

Teamwork

- Teamwork is linked to success in both the business and the academic worlds. As a group of learners, we represent a team. When your groups tackle an assignment, the group is functioning as a team as well. What five characteristics would you associate with the most effective teams?
- Should team leadership be rotated? Explain your answer.
- What is the worst team (instructional or work-related) you were ever part of? Describe what made the team ineffective.
- What is the supervisor's role as far as teams are concerned?
- In a setting like this, what is the instructor's role?
- What explains someone's ability to influence or persuade team members to accept an idea?
- What kinds of teams could you form with your co-workers to use what has been learned in this class?
- What are some effective ways of dealing with conflict within a team?

Energy Management

- Why do you think I asked one person from each team to move to a different team for the second half of the workshop?
- At what point in the course did you find your energy level lowest? Other than a break, what could have restored your energy level?
- Just to recharge your mental batteries, who can tell me what holiday is represented by the following combination of letters I have here on the flip chart?

  A B C D E F G H I J K M N O P Q R S T U V W X Y Z

  (The answer is "Christmas," because there is no L [Noel] in the list.)
- You might also suggest other mental problems, such as this one: There are eight supervisors (use the noun that relates to the attendees—nurses, engi-

neers, ABC employees, etc.) in a room. Each one shakes hands just once with each of the other supervisors. What is the total number of handshakes? (The answer is 28.)

- Why do you think "energy" keeps popping up on the list of leadership attributes?

- Do you know how to "nose write"?[1]

Knowledge Transfer

- Can you and your team list twenty things that you recall learning here? It could be facts, figures, names, or steps in a process.

- Now can you categorize the items on your list?

- I have listed the ten concepts I believe are most critical to understanding this topic. Which do you understand and which do you need to understand better?

- Assume that your life depends on having individuals on your team demonstrate complete understanding of each of these terms. Find out who on your team knows what by asking questions of others so that, when called on, your team can demonstrate mastery of each term.

Closure

- What stands out in your mind as the most valuable information you acquired in this course?

- If I asked you to come back and present a ten-minute "lesson" to the next class, what topic would you select and how would you present it?

- Can you name one key concept from each segment in the instructional outline?

- What advice can you give me to make this class even better the next time it is presented?

- Will you share with your supervisor and your co-workers some of the things you have learned? If so, what and when?

---

[1]Nose-writing is a quick stress-reduction technique. Demonstrate it by removing your glasses (if you wear them) and pretending to spell out your first name in large capital letters by using your nose as a pencil. Make your movements bold and pronounced. Nose writing usually elicits laughter, but more importantly it loosens up tight muscles in the neck and shoulder areas that are not usually reached by a simple head-rotation movement. Give participants a few minutes to practice the technique themselves.

- If this class had a final exam, what questions should be part of it?
- Have we met our objectives? Explain your answer.
- If your supervisor asked you for a two-minute report on what you learned, what would you say?
- In what ways are you different from the way you were when you walked in here at the start of this class?

Retention/Application

- If I were to contact you in two weeks and ask what you were doing differently as a result of attending this class, what would you be likely to tell me?
- The organization has made quite an investment in you by sending you to this training session. What return can you give them on this investment?
- What specific support or support systems would work best in helping you to use what you have learned?
- Assume that your manager is going to be called in a month and asked to describe any changes in your work behavior as a result of your taking this class. What changes would he or she be likely to notice?

TYPES OF QUESTIONS

Many types of questions are available to the trainer in search of excellence. The four most valuable are noted here, beginning with a construct that has six questions within it.

Bloom's Taxonomy

Benjamin Bloom of the University of Chicago remains unchallenged with the structure he proposed for questioning. His *Taxonomy of Educational Objectives* (1956) has guided instructional interactions for decades. The six levels are listed below, along with an illustrative question for each.

- *Knowledge:* "Who is known as the father of modern management science?"
- *Comprehension:* "How would you explain the meaning of this Sam Walton quote?"
- *Application:* "How would you use active listening in a conflict situation?"

- *Analysis:* "What conclusions can you draw from this case study?"

- *Synthesis:* "Having learned about Jack Welch's insistence on 'speed, simplicity, self-confidence,' what comparable statement can you make about the needs of your own organization?"

- *Evaluation:* "Can you tell us which of these statements is more relevant for the empowerment project your team is likely to undertake: 'Make no small plans for they have no power to stir the soul' (Anonymous), or 'We can do no great things, only small things with great love' (Mother Theresa)?"

Energizing Questions

Some questions should be asked of the group as a whole, especially those that require considerable speculation and discussion among participants. One such question could be, "Harvey Mackay, CEO of a multimillion-dollar manufacturing company, personally hires just one employee. Who do you think that is?" (The answer is "the receptionist.") Keeping abreast of current business events will enable you to formulate such questions and to use them as bridges to relevant curricular issues.

Transition Questions

Transition questions have many uses. At the beginning of a class, when you wish to start on time, but you realize five or six participants have not yet arrived, use a transition question to meet your prompt-start objective, but also to delay the "official" opening of the class. Use such questions, too, when you have a few minutes left before lunch or a break. When you're about to begin an especially challenging module, ask transition questions to start "cerebral juices" flowing. Here are a few examples from a leadership session.

- "If leadership (or whatever the topic is) were a color, what color would it be and why?"

- "How many words that start with an 'L' can you think of that relate to leadership?"

- "What vehicle would you select to describe the leadership of your organization?"

- "When you hear the word 'leadership,' who springs to mind?"

Speculative Questions

If we do not allow participants some time to internalize the learning, to view it from new perspectives, to push it into unexplored mental terrain, then we do them a disservice. Questions can be so intriguing that attendees will return to them again and again. Speculative questions can truly shatter mental constructs, and narrow views can be broadened to encompass original thought. Sample questions are provided below.

- "If you were arrested for leadership, what answers would you give to what questions from a prosecutor trying to convict you?"
- "If money were no object, what changes would you make in your workplace?"
- "Regarding the work environment, what lights your fire? What burns you up?"
- "If the CEO of your company switched roles with you for just one day, what would he or she learn about you and the work you are required to do?"
- "What questions about leadership are you unable to answer?"
- "What conclusions would Carl Jung have reached if he had been able to study the leadership of your organization?"
- "What would it take to make your work team eligible for the Organizational Olympics?"

CONCLUSION

If Peter Drucker was right, and if we wish to enhance leadership in ourselves and others, then enhancing our questioning process is a must. Trainers, as influencers of the thought process, must do more than put forth impromptu and unplanned verbal challenges. We need both to demonstrate and to develop leadership by asking the "right" questions—those that probe and prod and prompt and pique; those that challenge and change and stimulate creativity; those that, in short, make the learning experience the best it can be.

References

Bloom, B. (1956). *Taxonomy of educational objectives.* New York: David McKay.

Tuckman, B.W., & Jensen, M.A.C. (1977). Stages of small-group development revisited. *Group and Organization Studies, 2*(4), 419–427.

***Marlene Caroselli, Ed.D.**, directs the Center for Professional Development, started in 1984 to assist working adults develop their leadership, management, and communication skills. Her clients include both small and Fortune 100 companies, state and federal governments, and educational institutions. She presents seminars and keynote addresses nationally and internationally, and is the author of thirty-six books. Additionally, she contributes frequently to the* National Business Employment Weekly, The International Customer Service Association Journal, *and Stephen Covey's* Executive Excellence.

THE CUSTOMER MIND READER:
SECRETS OF UNDERSTANDING YOUR CUSTOMER

Peter R. Garber

Abstract: This article is intended to be used as a
primer for customer service representatives, but it
is also useful as a handout in training all members
of an organization to give high-quality service to
both internal and external customers. It is written
in simple, conversational language and deals with
common service situations. Its premise is that customers often behave as if service representatives
should be able to read their minds, and the author
offers seven secrets of "mind reading."

$\mathbf{H}$ave you ever thought to yourself, "What does my customer expect me to do—read his or her mind"? For most people who serve customers, the answer to this question is undoubtedly "yes." Sometimes, to provide the level of service customers expect, you must be able to anticipate what they want before even they know they want it!

Of course, none of us can actually read the customers' minds, and your customer service training did not come equipped with a crystal ball to gaze into the future. However, there are ways that we can better understand and predict what the customers' requirements and needs may be in the future. All of us serve customers—internal and external. We can all benefit by learning to be a customer service mind reader. We can all learn to read and to understand the messages customers send.

Imagine that this article is an old dusty book you just found on a shelf hidden away that contains seven lost secrets about how to understand customers. These "secrets" may seem surprisingly simple, but they can help you have a distinct advantage over your competition.

Let's explore the seven secrets displayed in Figure 1.

Secret 1: Study Your Customers' Past Buying Habits

Identify your customers' behavior patterns. Observe how they react in a variety of situations. Then watch for the emerging patterns. People generally behave in ways that have worked effectively for them in the past. If a particular response or behavior has had favorable results in prior situations, it is likely

---

1. Study your customers' past buying habits

2. Listen closely to the whole message

3. Listen with your eyes

4. Help your customers read their own minds

5. Make sure you are equipped with knowledge

6. Think like your customers do

7. Ask your customer for feedback

Figure 1. The Seven Secrets of Reading Customers' Minds

to be repeated in the future. For example, if a customer has had a problem corrected by becoming upset, you can expect the same behavior if you ever fail to meet requirements in the future!

Being able to predict this behavior can be very helpful. Planning what you will say to an angry customer to correct the problem before you are attacked increases your chances of turning a negative situation into a positive one.

When you have identified your customers' previous behaviors, you will be able to anticipate their objections before you are confronted with them. Assume, for example, that you have a customer who always needs to research all available data thoroughly before making a commitment. Also, you know that trying to accelerate the buying process would only strain your relationship with the customer. If you were planning a presentation for this customer, what predictions could you make about the customer's expected reactions? One such prediction might be that the customer will request time and additional information before making a decision.

By thinking in this way, you are "reading" the customer's mind. You can already predict a reaction before you make your presentation. You may even know some customers better than they know themselves! Instead of attempting to close the sale at the conclusion of your presentation as you might typically have done, you can give the customer all the data you have available and establish a time for the next contact. This approach can save both of you from being frustrated. You are not trying to convince the customer to make a decision before he or she is ready. The customer will appreciate your respect and sensitivity for his or her needs. Your relationship will become stronger and the possibility of making the sale will be enhanced—all because you took the effort to "read" your customer's mind to determine the best presentation approach.

Secret 2: Listen Closely to the Whole Message

If you listen closely enough, your customers will tell you how best to get and keep their business. This goes beyond just hearing what they are saying—and really listening. Unfortunately, there are many barriers to effective listening that make this objective very hard to achieve.

As humans we have the capacity to hear and comprehend nearly 1,000 words per minute. However, most people speak at a rate of 150 to 200 words per minute. This gives all of us a lot of extra time! What do you do with this extra time? Do you go on mental journeys or do you focus on what your customers are trying to tell you? We all have a tendency to think about what we are going to say next; we rehearse and refine our responses. The problem with these practice excursions is that we miss critically important indicators that provide insight into the speaker's thoughts and feelings. Customer mind reading requires a complete focus on what the customer is saying. The customer may be sending subtle messages that indicate what is really on his or her mind.

For example, a brief passing comment may be an early indication that the customer is looking for a different supplier. The customer may want to give you a warning—albeit a subtle one—that your business relationship is in jeopardy. You may not realize until it is too late what the customer was trying to tell you. The better listener you become, the more you will be able to "read" what is on your customer's mind and keep his or her business.

This same process can be used to identify the kind of relationship your customer wants with you. Some customers want to build a strong business relationship with their suppliers. Others want you to take up as little of their time as possible. The customer in one way or another will tell you these things if you listen closely enough.

Secret 3: Listen with Your Eyes

You might be thinking that there must be a misprint in the heading above. There is no misprint; we do listen with our eyes. In fact, in most interpersonal communications about 55 percent of the message received is nonverbal, 38 percent is from vocal inflections, and only 7 percent from the actual words spoken (Mehrabian, 1971). The problem is that most of us focus more on the words than on *how* they are said. The real communication is in the way we give the presentation, rather than the presentation itself. The same is also true when listening to a customer. It is not enough to simply focus on what the customer says, but more importantly *how* he or she says it. The customer's nonverbal signals and vocal inflections are the best indicators concerning what is really going on in his or her mind. For example, if your customer's arms are crossed against his or her chest, you might interpret this body language to mean that the customer is resistant to your message. If the customer is smiling and nodding, you might interpret that to mean agreement with your message.

This same principle is true when talking to a customer on the telephone. Approximately 88 percent of the real message is found in the person's vocal inflections. Again, listen not only to what the customer is saying but to how he or she says it! The customer's words might indicate that there are no problems with the quality of your service, but vocal inflections may send another message. You will need to further investigate the situation and the real meaning behind the words.

Secret 4: Help Your Customers Read Their Own Minds

Sometimes you need to help your customers read their own minds to understand what they really want. A customer may think and say one thing when in reality he or she requires something quite different.

For example, a customer may say that what he or she needs most is fast turnaround. However, after exploring the customer's requirements you might find that what he or she deems most important is not fast turnaround but error-free quality. In this case you need to find a way to communicate this insight to the customer.

An effective way to convey your understanding is to use reflective communication techniques. Simply reflect what the customer is saying. As the name of this technique implies, you serve as a mirror, "reflecting" the customer's thoughts and perceptions by paraphrasing his or her statements. For example, an important customer may say to you, "I need to have the highest quality product you can deliver with minimal lead time, and I do not want to pay overtime to meet the deadline." You might reflect by saying, "I hear that you want flawless quality and it is critically important to you that we be able to help you on a moment's notice. However, staying under budget is also an important factor, possibly even more important than the level of quality and service you've described. Is that correct?"

The customer may reply, "Yes, we do need a nearly perfect product, high quality, and we do need very tight delivery schedules because we won't have all the data until the last minute. However, if we need to hire temporary help to meet the delivery deadline, we're willing to do that. But we need to keep the cost as low as possible." The customer's response clarifies his or her meaning and intent.

Now both you and the customer know what is really important and what is required to maintain the relationship. At first, this customer asked for things that were potentially mutually exclusive and not really reasonable: highest quality, fast turnaround, and lowest cost. As it turned out, quality and delivery were the most important issues.

Secret 5: Make Sure You Are Equipped with Knowledge

Customers expect a lot today in terms of service and quality. One of these expectations is that those who provide customer service should know outcomes and consequences before they actually happen! For example, external customers would like you to predict when the markets they serve are about to change or what new products their competition is about to introduce. Internal customers may expect you to keep them informed about other departments' activities.

At the very least your customer expects you to know everything about your products or services. You do need to be knowledgeable about your processes and be able to prepare your customers for proposed changes and to explain the reasons for those changes.

Think back to circumstances in the past when a customer was disappointed in the quality of the service you provided. What were some of the reasons for this dissatisfaction? What could you have done to prevent these problems? What could you have learned that could have helped you reverse the situation and improve your relationship with the customer? What should you have known?

What else do your customers expect you to know? Where can you find this information? How could knowing this information help you provide better service to your customers?

Secret 6: Think Like Your Customers Do

Pretend you are one of your own customers. Try thinking the way your customers think. What would be important to you? What information would you seek? What feedback would you want to hear? What would influence you to be satisfied with the products and/or services you received?

Now mentally return to your own position of providing service to a specific customer. In interacting with this customer, how can you make use of what you learned by imagining yourself in the customer's situation? How can you let your customer know that you empathize with his or her needs?

Again, if you were the customer, what would build the greatest trust in the relationship? What can you do to begin strengthening this trust and providing better service to your customer?

Secret 7: Ask Your Customer for Feedback

Every provider of customer service would like to know how well he or she is meeting customer requirements. There are many ways you can elicit and receive this very important feedback. For instance, you could develop, administer, and analyze a customer survey. You could also ask for a meeting with each of several major customers to discuss ways in which you could better meet his or her needs. The most important factor is that you find out what is on your customer's mind.

Summary

You do not really have to be a mind reader to know what your customers are thinking. There are many ways to find out how customers feel about the quality of service you are providing. By asking for feedback, you can build stronger relationships with your customers, who will appreciate your concern about meeting their requirements.

Reading your customers' minds in this way does not require any mystical powers! Rather, simply demonstrate your concern and your dedication to providing the highest quality service possible.

Reference

Mehrabian, A. (1971). *Silent messages.* Belmont, CA: Wadsworth.

Peter R. Garber is manager of teamwork development for PPG Industries, Inc., in Pittsburgh, Pennsylvania. He is the author of a number of human resource and business related books, including Coaching Self-Directed Work Teams, Team Skillbuilders, 25 Customer Service Activities, 101 Ways to Build Better Relationships with Customers, *and* Managing by Remote Control. *He has also been a contributing author to the* Annual *for the past four years.*

USING THE INTERNET TO IDENTIFY TRAINING NEEDS

Brooke Broadbent

Abstract: This article illustrates how the Internet can help slice through international communication barriers. It examines how one Internet service, an electronic mailing list, can play a pivotal role in a global training-needs analysis. The article first explains what electronic mailing lists are and their benefits, then reveals the framework and the quantitative as well as the qualitative results of a training-needs analysis conducted via an electronic mailing list. The next segment proposes guidelines for reaping the benefits of electronic mailing lists and, in conclusion, the article offers tips garnered from lessons learned.

If you were to undertake a training-needs analysis to upgrade an existing global training program, how would you do it? Although a fact-finding intercontinental tour would be informative, or a meeting of people with experience with the existing program would be insightful, costs could be prohibitive. One obvious consideration is to use Internet e-mail. Communicating over the Internet eliminates travel costs, time zone concerns, and jet lag. It is fast and convenient—permitting users to access their e-mail when they choose. In the project discussed here, the team members are located on five continents, and they are competent computer users. The Internet, therefore, was a logical choice. The Internet service selected for this project was an electronic mailing list.

ELECTRONIC MAILING LISTS

Mailing lists permit the exchange of electronic mail messages, or e-mail, among people in a group. Regular e-mail software is used. However, whereas e-mail messages are typically sent to one other person or to a few selected individuals, mailing list messages normally are sent to all people who subscribe to the list.

Referred to as lists, mailing lists, Internet mailing lists, e-mail mailing lists, e-mail discussion groups, or LISTSERVS, electronic mailing lists are dynamic meeting places for the exchange of ideas, opinions, and information. Subscribers to mailing lists, also called members, help others solve problems, obtain information, and make contacts. Sometimes people confuse electronic mailing lists with chat groups or newsgroups, which require a participant to use specific software. Mailing lists, on the other hand, require subscribers to use their regular e-mail software. Chat discussions occur in "real time," whereas newsgroups and mailing list subscribers post messages that others read at their convenience. Another difference is that most mailing lists, especially public ones, are moderated, meaning that someone screens contributions. Chat groups and newsgroups are generally not moderated.

There are two types of mailing lists: private and public. Large public lists are often wide-angled, meaning that membership is unrestricted. They may have thousands of members and a daily torrent of messages. Private lists are often tightly focused. They may have only a handful of members and a trickle of messages. Membership is restricted. This article assumes the use of a private list, although the topics treated and conclusions drawn are also germane to public lists.

Advantages of Mailing Lists

Electronic mailing lists are a cost-effective way to bring people with common interests together. Benefits include the following:

1. Subscribers use their regular e-mail software, so if they know how to use e-mail, they can benefit from using a mailing list.

2. All contact is through the Internet, saving money on regular long-distance phone calls, conference calls, faxing, and travel.

3. The ability to attach documents to e-mail messages makes it easy to share files and other information.

4. In terms of sheer numbers, one can communicate with more people on an e-mail list than it would be possible to meet face-to-face.

5. Messages posted to the list can be archived on a centrally accessible Website and easily accessed by all subscribers using a Web browser.

6. Subscribers to a list can access list postings when it is convenient for them—an important factor with a global training-needs analysis project that crosses many time zones.

Information for Technophiles

This article is about using an electronic mailing list; however, if you are involved in setting up such a list, we have included a few introductory technical details here that will help you get started. Before setting up an Internet mailing list, you will need to find an Internet Service Provider (ISP) that offers a mailing list service. Fortunately, most do. The common mailing list software packages are Majordomo, ListProc, and LISTSERV. Your ISP determines which one you use. From the perspective of a user (a subscriber), these different programs perform similar functions. Moreover, they have similar commands for subscribing and unsubscribing—important commands to know. Explanations of key commands and other valuable information are normally conveyed by the list owner to list members when they subscribe.

Prerequisites: Equipment, Skills, and Attitude

The pieces of equipment that are essential for an individual subscriber to access a list are a computer or terminal, a modem, and a telephone line or another way of connecting to Internet services. Also, each subscriber must have regular access to Internet e-mail. Mailing lists operate on an array of diverse popular platforms, such as DOS, UNIX, Mac, and Windows. The skills and knowledge required of list members are those needed to compose e-mail messages: keyboarding, e-mail software knowledge, and the ability to write intelligible text in the language used by list members. As for attitudinal prerequisites, patience helps if there are glitches, as well as openness to new ways, and a willingness to abide by the rules governing Internet discussions.

RESULTS OF THE PROJECT

The framework of our effort to gather training needs data through an electronic mailing list are detailed below, highlighting quantitative results—the numbers and types of replies we gathered from the list. A review of qualitative results—the extent to which the process produced worthwhile information—is also given.

Discussion Framework

The purpose of our Internet-based discussions was to gather the data to write a comprehensive training-needs analysis report considering five areas: the context of the training, characteristics of the users of the training, the work being performed by the people taking the training, the content of the training courses, and the limits of the impact of training.

One typical question we asked in each of these areas is given below:

Context. "How much support will there be for this type of training?"

Characteristics of Users. "How do potential participants prefer to learn?"

Work Performed. "How will IDRC researchers use the information?"

Content. "What functions present a challenge to IDRC researchers?"

Limits of Training. "What issues inhibit IDRC researchers in using the knowledge or skills?"

The ultimate purpose for the needs analysis was to provide sufficient data to design training to develop the knowledge and skills for the International Development Research Centre (IDRC) researchers. The goal was to provide consistently effective and interactive training courses that would appeal to the widest possible audience.

We launched our electronic mailing list in mid-November 1997 with twelve subscribers. These people were picked for their knowledge of the existing training program that we were endeavoring to upgrade. Our subscribers were also selected based on their diverse locations on five continents, as well as the fact that they would be involved in the implementation of the final training. Our "volunteers" were extremely busy during the duration of the project. At least four were conducting courses. Four traveled internationally. List members were engaged in a wide variety of pursuits other than our e-mail discussion, so the discussion was, understandably, not always at the top of their to-do lists.

The electronic mailing list was active for approximately one month. As is most often the case with lists, ours was facilitated. We used two facilitators: the main one was the author, ably assisted by the client for the project.

Quantitative Results

We initiated the list with the assumption that subscribers would post two messages a week. In our case—a four-week period of discussion among twelve people—we expected around one hundred messages. Although we approached our quantitative goal, more than half of the postings came from the two facilitators of the list, who were struggling to foster discussion. Full participation was slow in coming. As a result the co-facilitators had several off-line discussions about whether the list would accomplish what we hoped to achieve in the one-month time frame.

As of mid-December, subscribers posted ninety-five messages. These treated a wide variety of topics related to training-needs analysis. In the main facilitator role, the author posted thirty-four of the messages. The co-facilitator of the project posted sixteen messages. The next most active participant posted eight messages. The majority of subscribers posted from two to five messages. Everyone posted at least one message.

The number of postings was lower than expected; however, their quality was high. The comprehensive content of postings indicated that members were "lurking" (reading messages but not responding). Lurking is quite accepted in the mailing list realm.

We posted a comprehensive questionnaire toward the end of our consultation, and it generated a 100 percent response rate. Nothing was unique about the questionnaire used for the needs analysis. The primary difference between it and other such questionnaires was that we skipped questions that had been answered during the initial Internet discussions and added areas that surfaced during those same discussions.

Qualitative Results

Despite our initial concerns about the quantity of messages posted, the final qualitative results were excellent. We gathered abundant information—in fact it was challenging to sort through the information and produce a final report. Some of the information we gathered could have been predicted. Some was surprising and contentious. One of the "sticky" issues was discussed at some length on the telephone between two of the leading list members. This might not have occurred as early in the process during a conventional needs analysis. The subscribers reached consensus on most issues, and in the few areas where they did not agree, they agreed to disagree.

One of the outstanding benefits of conducting a training-needs analysis this way is that participants—the same people who will carry the training program forward—understand the reasoning behind the approach. In this case, they witnessed the program and its rationale unfold during our mailing list discussions.

PROJECT SUMMARY

We carried out a world-wide consultation with the people who would be using the training materials we would develop during a later phase. We achieved the goals set for the project. We amassed abundant data from which we wrote a comprehensive training-needs analysis report. A side benefit was that we eliminated travel costs. The report became the foundation for developing a two-and-a-half-year training plan, now used globally.

In the course of doing our project, we found that an electronic mailing list was a viable vehicle for conducting a training-needs analysis. We did, however, face challenges. We learned that the absence of opportunities for nonverbal communication lessened the influence of the facilitators. More attention was required for written communication to compensate for the absence of nonverbal communication.

Based on our experience, it seems that using electronic means may take longer and take more effort to conduct a training-needs analysis than do using focus groups, interviews, questionnaires, and other data-collection methods. Each of these methods has its strong points, and any decisions about which to use should be viewed from that perspective. The face-to-face immediacy of focus groups, for example, allows a level of interaction and synergy that will probably never be achieved with an electronic mailing list.

TIPS FOR CONDUCTING A TRAINING-NEEDS ANALYSIS ON THE INTERNET

Although we considered the project a success, there were challenges along the way. We hope that discussing the pitfalls we faced and actions we took will help readers to approach similar projects realistically and with common sense strategies.

At the outset of the discussions, we relied on techniques normally used to facilitate focus groups face-to-face (Broadbent, 1997b). As discussion progressed, we realized that managing discussion and sharing information through an electronic mailing list is quite different from doing it in person. Although we had set an agenda with topics and time frames, members did not follow it, and we had no way to bring discussion back to our plan. In a meeting of a training-needs focus group, the facilitator can post the agenda, glance at a clock, use other nonverbal cues, call "time out" to review what has been accomplished so far, or highlight what remains to be accomplished. An electronic mailing list does not afford similar opportunities to capture the attention of the group and refocus people. Our participants, like members of any mailing list, accessed their messages when they wished, chose which messages to read, and selected which messages they would respond to. As facilitators of a group of far-flung volunteers, we did not "control" the discussion. We did, however, exercise influence through facilitation techniques, as explained below.

Facilitating a List with Kick-Off Messages

The initial postings from the list facilitator will set the tone for later interaction among subscribers. Keep the initial posting short and clear. Based on our experience, facilitators should send the following four types of messages separately, inviting responses from list members:

1. A message to let participants know when the list will be ready and to tell people how to subscribe, or advising people that you have already added them to the list, as the case may be.

2. A welcoming message explaining the purpose of the list and administrative matters such as unsubscribing, subscribing to various formats, ground rules, and other important information, such as how to access the list archives.

3. A "Hello, I am . . ." message, by which facilitators present themselves and invite others to do the same—with relevant professional and perhaps some personal information.

4. A short, initial question to quick-start dialogue about the topics to be discussed.

Using Summaries and Questions

In terms of expediting discussion, two actions we took seemed to help. First, by summarizing discussions to date, facilitators were able to update members, especially those who joined us in the midst of our discussion. Participants voiced their appreciation for our summaries. Second, we channeled discussion through an extensive online questionnaire. We had planned a questionnaire from the beginning and advised subscribers with our first posting. Questions in the survey reflected those normally asked in a training-needs analysis process (Broadbent, 1998). In all, there were fifty-seven questions, broken down as follows:

- Context: 19,
- Content: 7,
- Materials: 6,
- Instructors: 1, and
- Objectives: 24.

All participants responded to this questionnaire (with some prodding and encouraging), and their statements provided the bulk of information for our final report.

Facilitating

Online discussions require planning, prompting, reviewing, and skillful facilitation. Facilitators can use some of the same techniques they would use when facilitating a focus group by doing the following:

1. Lay out an agenda and expectations for the entire discussion, including goals, roles, and time frames.
2. Welcome members as they introduce themselves.
3. Provide guidelines similar to those in Figure 1 to members new to the process.
4. Initiate discussion on specific points.
5. Summarize discussions so that new members can catch up.
6. Invite participation from all members.
7. Thank people for their participation.
8. Forge a consensus.
9. Prepare a final report of the project.

Co-Facilitating

Although individual facilitators may have considerable experience as members of electronic mailing lists, they may be thrown a few unexpected curve balls as facilitators. In such cases, working with a co-facilitator may be helpful. It is reassuring to debate strategies and to tweak your thinking outside of the public discussion. Having a co-facilitator may make it possible to develop innovative approaches, shape the discussion, and achieve your goals in a shorter period of time.

CONCLUSION

List technology is readily available. It saves money. It produces results. It could be worth trying the next time you conduct a training-needs analysis with a geographically dispersed group of people who are computer literate. But mailing lists are not a panacea for cutting training-needs analysis costs. Never use a list because it is new technology that you want to try. Do use a list to save travel costs, or use an electronic mailing list to foster ongoing discussion.

The following guidelines provide ideas for how list members can receive maximum benefits from an electronic mailing list. They are based on resources readily available on the Internet and often described as "netiquette."

1. Introduce yourself in your first posting.

2. Keep postings concise—ideally not exceeding two screens.

3. Keep sentences and paragraphs short and to the point.

4. When responding to a message, retain the original subject heading so that recipients can follow a thread, unless you are changing the subject.

5. Always include a pertinent subject title for the message so that recipients can locate the message quickly.

6. Never send any messages that you would not mind seeing on the evening news.

7. Avoid capitalizing, as this is generally considered to be the Net equivalent of SHOUTING!

8. Include your signature at the bottom of messages as well as your other contact information.

9. Do not use sarcasm, rudeness (flames), or complex humor. Without face-to-face communication, your jokes may be viewed as criticism.

10. Remember that mailing lists have worldwide membership. Do not assume that people will understand your references to television, sports, pop culture, or current events in your own country.

11. Follow all guidelines that the list coordinator or "owner" has posted as local "netiquette" standards for the list.

12. Do not keep the body of the original text in your replies, except as absolutely necessary, as the more text in a message, the longer it takes to download and the longer recipients have to stay connected to their ISP. The longer one is connected to an ISP, the greater the telecommunication and ISP charges.

13. Find out if there is a FAQ list (frequently asked questions, with answers) for a list you join. If there is, consult it. You might be pleasantly surprised by the wealth of information the FAQ contains.

Figure 1. Mailing List Guidelines

Remember that it is challenging to lead a list discussion. A facilitator must have high-level writing skills and finely tuned facilitation skills. You might find that a combination of methods has merit. For instance, an initial focus-group meeting, conference call, or video conference could launch a training-needs analysis project. An electronic mailing list could then be used to continue discussions.

Although our project was specifically designed to conduct a training-needs analysis, the process could be used to gather other types of information as well. For example, an organization may want to identify material resources or individuals who have specific areas of expertise.

If you use a mailing list for whatever reason, keep in mind the extra burden and time that using such a list places on facilitators. Give yourself plenty of time to start and complete your list-based discussion. With a small amount of planning, using the Internet can be an effective tool to gather data from individuals who are geographically dispersed. It can save time, reduce costs, and achieve a high percentage of involvement.

References

Broadbent, B. (1997a, August). Lessons learned: Designing training to teach computer applications. *Performance Improvement*, pp. 14-15.

Broadbent, B. (1997b). Twelve steps to successful focus group meetings. In M. Silberman (Ed.), the *1997 McGraw-Hill team and organization development sourcebook*. New York: McGraw-Hill.

Broadbent, B. (1998). *Using the Internet: Smarter and faster.* (1998). Los Altos, CA: Crisp.

Broadbent, B., & Froidevaux, L. (1998) Training-needs analysis: A broad view. In *The 1998 annual: Vol. 1, training.* San Francisco, CA: Jossey-Bass/Pfeiffer.

James, M., & Rykert, L. (1998). *From workplace to work space: Using e-mail lists to work together.* Ottawa, Ontario, Canada: The International Development Research Centre.

Weiss, E. (1997). *The accidental trainer.* San Francisco, CA: Jossey-Bass.

For more information about public mailing lists point your browser to:

http://www.liszt.com
http://www.neosoft.com/internet/paml

For more information about Canada's International Development Research Centre and this project, try:

GOTOBUTTON BM_1_ http://www.idrc.ca/unganisha/

Brooke Broadbent *is a writer, trainer, and instructional designer. He has extensive experience throughout North America, Europe, Asia, and Africa designing
and conducting training. When he is not conducting train-the-trainer workshops,
Brooke is cobbling together training programs and crafting books. His latest book
is* Using the Internet: Smarter and Faster.

MEDIA SELECTION REVISITED: TRAINING IN THE AGE OF INTERACTIVE TECHNOLOGY

Zane L. Berge

Abstract: In an era in which the demand for training and lifelong learning is continually increasing, how can we best use existing and new technologies in the service of teaching and learning? When can training be enhanced by the use of technologies beyond the stand-up lecture in a training room? How can we best select the media to match the instructional objectives and goals for training programs?

A great many factors could be used for classifying media and for selecting media for a given training program. Probably the single most important principle is that a mix of approaches is best, as no single technology fits all training situations. It is assumed here that decisions about pedagogy should be made first, and then decisions made about appropriate media (Romiszowski, 1988). Regrettably, the availability and cost of various technologies is often the deciding factor.

This article identifies common educational technologies used in training and predicts, on the basis of several surveys, the trends that will be prevalent over the next several years. The author also discusses some of the key factors in media selection from the designer's perspective.

EDUCATIONAL TECHNOLOGY

Businesses are no longer relying solely on face-to-face, teacher-led, training-room instruction. A wide variety of common technologies are already in use for training. Videoconferencing, the Internet, CD-ROMs, interactive multi-media, audiotapes, and computer conferencing are all used to link learners to content, instructors, and other trainees. Whatever the technology chosen, under many conditions it can make training easier, faster, and cheaper than traditional instructor-led sessions.

In order to assist in program planning for the Training Systems Graduate Program at the University of Maryland Baltimore County, regional trainers and users of educational technology were surveyed regarding their current use of technology and those they planned to use in the future. Results of this survey were compared with results of national surveys to determine whether there were regional differences. A complete report of the results and limitations of this study is available on the Web at *http://www.gl.umbc.edu/~berge/edtchsrv.html* or by contacting the author. A subset of the analyses is reported here to indicate the scope and some possible trends in the use of educational technology in training, with particular emphasis on technology that leads to interactive participation between teacher and learner and among learners.

In analyzing the differences among the types of media and delivery methods that are currently used by survey respondents and their projections for three years from now, several trends appear to be significant (see Appendix A for brief definitions of the media and terms). Table 1 lists the differences for both instructor-led courses and distance/distributed classes.

As can be seen from the table, respondents predicted that in three years, videoconferencing will be used 28.5 percent more often than it is today in teacher-led courses, but 6.5 percent less in distance courses. According to the respondents to this survey, the use of lectures and overhead transparencies in teacher-led courses seem to be diminishing, while the use of videoconferencing is increasing. In distance/distributed classes, not surprisingly, the largest increases are predicted to be in the use of the Internet and intranets. Additionally, gains are projected for the use of workbooks and manuals, noncomputerized self-study programs, desktop videoconferencing, and computer-based training and multimedia.

**Table 1. Differences Between Current and Projected Use
of Types of Media in Training**

Types of Media and Delivery	Projected Use in Three Years vs. Current Use	
	Teacher-Led Courses	Distance Classes
Audio cassettes	6.5	− 9.7
Business books	− 3.2	0
Case studies	− 12.9	6.4
CD–ROM	16.1	3.3
Commercial satellite distance learning	12.9	12.9
Company-owned satellite distance learning	9.7	3.3
Computer-based training/multimedia	9.7	− 9.7
Desktop videoconferencing	16.1	19.4
EPSS	19.3	12.9
Games and simulations	− 6.5	16.1
Instructor-led classes (lectures)	− 16.1	9.7
Noncomputerized self-study programs	16.1	19.3
Overheads/transparencies	− 19.4	− 3.2
Role plays	− 3.2	0
Self-assessment tools	− 9.7	− 3.0
Slides	− 9.6	− 3.3
Videoconferencing	28.5	− 6.5
Videotapes	− 12.9	− 6.4
Virtual reality	19.4	16.1
Workbooks/manuals	− 6.4	22.6
World Wide Web/Internet	16.1	29.0
Your organization's intranet	19.3	29.0

The trend toward increasing the use of the Internet and intranets for training delivery seems consistent with other surveys, most notably the Survey of Educational Technology published by the Federal Aviation Administration (FAA) (1996) and the results published by the American Society for Training and Development (ASTD) (1997). The ASTD survey states that 12 percent of their Benchmarking Forum companies were using Internet- or network-based electronic distance learning in 1994, 33 percent in 1995, and over half (53 percent) in 1996. Eighty-one percent of these companies anticipated an increased use of the Internet for internal training in the next three years (Bassi, Cheney, & Van Buren, 1997). Similarly, the FAA survey executive summary states, "the Internet is considered an exciting training option and is predicted to be the distance training choice of the future" (1996, p. 3).

Given the plethora of technologies to choose from, how *should* one select appropriate media for training delivery? What follows is a model from the trainer's or instructional designer's perspective. It sets aside the practical constraints, both administrative and economic, that are always significant within training systems. Essentially, *media are selected from a trainer's perspective on the basis of teaching method.* Teaching methods are in large part a function of the synchronization and level of performance that are desired for the particular instructional goals of the program and also a function of the instructor's personal teaching philosophy.

MEDIA SELECTION FROM AN INSTRUCTIONAL PERSPECTIVE

In general, after conducting an analysis of the training situation (e.g., learner characteristics, learning environment, job or task analyses, etc.), instructional designers and trainers begin to think about how to convert the skills and knowledge that are required for mastery of the instructional goals into practice activities to engage the learner and facilitate learning. As the list of possible activities evolves, what technology or media will support these activities?

Some factors that are important for designing effective instruction include: any special physical or other disabilities that characterize the learner; whether learners are in a large group, small groups, or involved with individual study; suitability for stable subject matter or for subject matter that often changes; learner control; the number of learners; the location of the learners; learning styles; teaching styles; current infrastructure; number of locations; compatibility of systems; and sharing resources to maximize existing investments (e.g., collaboration between government agencies, corporate organizations, and academia could make educational technology very cost-effective and reduce the overall start-up costs for any one organization). Among the key factors in media selection are three: level of performance required by the instructional goals of the program, instructional methods selected to support performance, and the synchronization permitted by a particular medium.

Level of Performance

Although program content or subject matter may influence media selection, the learning objectives determined by the initial analysis will also impact the choice, because those objectives will dictate or limit the *methods* of instruction. The tasks assigned to the learners are, in part, a function of the level of performance the trainer seeks from the learner.

In Table 2, the instructor-controlled level of performance (either cognitive or physical skills or knowledge) connotes learning that is didactic, completely guided, generally deductive, introductory, and informing. (It is similar to Bloom's [1956] "knowledge" category or Gagné's [1985] "know," or Tennyson's [1992] "declarative knowledge.") The guided learner-controlled level is generally inductive, guided, drill/practice/apply, and somewhat contrived. (It is similar to what Bloom called "application" or Gagné categorized as "use," or Tennyson's "procedural knowledge."). The learner-controlled level of skill is inductive, experimental, problem-centered, culminating, realistic, and complete. (It corresponds roughly to what Bloom categorized as "analysis," "synthesis," and "evaluation," or Gagné called "find," or Tennyson's "contextual knowledge.")

Instructional Methods

Instructors' implicit or explicit personal philosophies of what constitutes good instruction impact their choice of teaching methods. Some instructors view content as a body of facts, concepts, principles, or attitudes to be transmitted to the learner in some way. Other instructors believe learning is a transformation and that each learner constructs his or her own knowledge. If instructors' beliefs about the importance of social learning are taken into account, there is great diversity possible. To learner-centered instructors, part of "teaching well" is encouraging self-direction and learner control. Learner-centered instructors use a broad spectrum of teaching methods to accomplish their goals. Figure 1 lists teaching methods on a spectrum from instructor-focused to learner-focused. Instructors tend to select teaching devices, methods and techniques, and communication and media channels that are consistent with their personal philosophies.

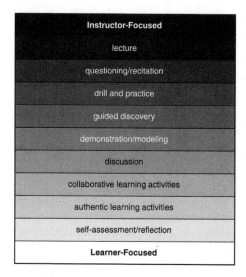

Figure 1. Continuum of Teaching Methods

Synchronous and Asynchronous Communication

Synchronous communication occurs in real time, for example, in a course delivered in a classroom or via video or audio conferencing. All participants must be present, although not necessarily at the same physical location. *Asynchronous* communication between learners and instructor is in some way technologically mediated, but is *not* dependent on the learner(s) and instructor being together at a specific time or location. Besides the convenience to learners of being able to work when and where they want, with asynchronous methods learners can also control the pace of their learning (Berge, 1996).

Real-time and asynchronous communication channels often serve different purposes or are used for solving different instructional problems. For instance, real-time, two-way video usually is more efficient than asynchronous discussion for team-building activities. For team building, synchronous methods may be important for such things as forming a common understanding, indoctrinating into the culture of the organization, and for more immediate feedback to the instructor from the trainees. On the other hand, asynchronous computer conferencing allows participants time to reflect on their responses to questions posed (Berge, 1994).

Media Selection As a Function of Synchronization and Level of Performance

Table 2 shows media possibilities for given teaching methods as a function of the levels of synchronization and performance desired. The list is not exhaustive, but serves to show that level of performance and teaching methods must match. The table shows only one medium for any given instructional method. In fact, there are usually quite a few that could be used. Of course, there are practical and economic considerations that also limit media selection in addition to the learner outcomes desired.

**Table 2. Media Selection As a Function
of Synchronization and Level of Performance**

		Communication Mode	
		Synchronous	**Asynchronous**
Level of Performance	**Instructor-Controlled**	• Lecture (technologically mediated through television or radio or other media) • Question/recitation (e.g., television with two-way audio; two-way TV)	• Assigned readings (e.g.,textbooks, documents on the Web) • Demonstration (e.g.,videotape, slides, video streaming)
	Guided Learner-Controlled	• Annotated problem solving (e.g., fax, videoconferencing, audiographics) • Self-contained, case study (e.g., audio-conferencing) • Role play (e.g., phone, videoconferencing)	• Tutorials (e.g., CBT, audiotape) • Guided simulations (e.g., CBT, CD-ROM, virtual reality, intranet) • Team inquiry (e.g., computer conferencing)
	Learner-Controlled	• Original problem solving (e.g., Internet, CBT) • Open-ended case study (e.g., computer conferencing)	• Open-ended case study (commercial electronic databases, Internet) • Reflection (e.g., computerized self-assessment tools)

Summary

When selecting media for training, those closest to the implementation are likely to choose technology intuitively that will allow them to use their preferred teaching styles. Unfortunately, it is often the case that the decision makers are not very close to implementation and choose only to consider existing infrastructure and costs, rather than learning goals. The simple model presented here suggests that the media used in training should be directly linked with the learning outcomes of the program.

References

American Society for Training and Development. (1997). *Percent of companies using selected delivery systems (1994-1996).* http:astd.org/who/research/bench-mar/96stats/graph13.gif

Bassi, L.J., Cheney, S., & Van Buren, M. (1997, November). Training industry trends 1997. *Training & Development,* pp. 46–59.

Berge, Z.L. (1994). Electronic discussion groups. *Communication Education, 43*(2), 102–111.

Berge, Z.L. (1996, Summer). Where interaction intersects time. *MC Journal: The Journal of Academic Media Librarianship, 4*(1), 69–83. http://wings.buffalo. edu/publications/mcjrnl/v4n1/berge.html#mk

Bloom, B.S. (1956). *Taxonomy of educational objectives handbook 1: The cognitive domain.* New York: David McKay.

Borich, G.D. (1996). *Effective teaching methods* (3rd ed.). Englewood Cliffs, NJ: Merrill.

Federal Aviation Administration. (1996). *Survey of educational technology.* Washington, DC: Training Program Office, AHR-14.

Gagné, R. (1985). *The conditions of learning* (4th ed.). New York: Holt, Rinehart & Winston.

Romiszowski, A.J. (1988). *The selection and use of instructional media* (2nd ed.). New York: Kogan Page.

Tennyson, R.D. (1992, January). An educational learning theory for instructional design. *Educational Technology,* pp. 36–41.

Zane L. Berge, Ph.D., *is widely published in the field of computer-mediated communication used for teaching and learning, most notably,* Computer-Mediated Communication and the Online Training Room, Volumes 1 through 3 *(1995) and a four-volume series,* Wired Together: Computer Mediated Communication in the K-12 Training Room *(1998). Dr. Berge is director of the graduate program in training systems at the University of Maryland Baltimore County. He consults and conducts research internationally in distance education.*

Appendix A

Glossary

CD-ROM. High capacity, laser read, digital data storage disks in CD format that may contain text, visuals, and/or sound. They are accessed by computer.

Computer-Based Training (CBT). Individualized training delivered through a computer application.

Desktop Video Conferencing. Video conferencing that takes place on a personal computer.

Distance Training (DT). Learning by some or all trainees that takes place at locations or times separate from the instructor and/or other trainees. For example, an instructor-led course may be delivered to other locations by satellite, or students at different sites may receive training applications through computer networks.

Electronic Performance Support System (EPSS). Computer-based systems that provide the user with quick access to assistance with minimum support from other people.

Instructor-Led (or Teacher-Led) Training. An instructor leads the training through lecture, printed manuals or workbooks, role plays, or similar traditional methods.

Internet/World Wide Web (WWW). An immense system of computer networks that allows people at many different locations to interact with one another and share electronic information.

Intranet. An organization-wide information system that often connects to the Internet.

Multimedia-Based Training. A learning experience that incorporates multiple types of media, usually either CD-ROM or World Wide Web technology.

Video Conferencing. Joining two or more groups at different locations using a combination of video and audio equipment that may include an exchange of graphics and data.

Virtual Reality (VR). A multimedia environment that simulates a 3-D, multisensory event.

TEAM TRAINING:
FACILITATING REAL-TIME TEAM LEARNING

Emile A. Robert, Jr., and Barbara Pate Glacel

Abstract: Team members need training in team skills in order to ensure the enhanced performance available from the interdependence of people with complementary skills. However, time to provide training is usually at a premium. Utilizing real-time experiences and facilitated reflection allows team learning to be ongoing. Teams must perform the basic behaviors of investing time, gaining participation, and managing differences in order to achieve results. These are behaviors which, through facilitated reflection, can enhance team performance.

THE DEMAND FOR REAL-TIME TRAINING

Skeptics sometimes question the value of training. Given the rapidly changing needs and demands of organizations, perhaps the skepticism is healthy. Where does one find the time, money, and energy to send employees off to training that may or may not be relevant? But, if training—at least the conventional type of classroom training—does not meet the needs of today's organizations, how can individuals, teams, and organizations learn and change to keep up with those very demands that get in the way of finding time for training? Sounds like a circular argument, doesn't it?

If classroom training is an anachronism, what is needed is real-time, immediate training in actual business settings or in a close simulation of the business setting. Organizations need ongoing, real-time training that constantly raises the bar for performance standards for individuals, teams, and the organization as a whole. Real-time training must allow learning from the successes and failures of current practices. If training cannot meet that need, the organization will fail to survive in the global competition today, much less tomorrow.

If this premise makes sense to you, you might then ask, "Who will do the training?" Who is this all-time wise person who has the answers to organizational and business success? Strangely enough, the answer is found in the very individuals and teams who require the training. Yet, perhaps these "experts" are too close to the demands and problems at hand to see the answers. What they need is a translator, a tour guide, a facilitator to aid in the process of real-time learning.

Substitute "learning" for "training" and "facilitator" for "trainer," and you have the answer for all those skeptics who question the value of training in organizations. The answer is clearly an imperative. Learn (read "train") or die in the organizational environment, be it a business, not-for-profit, government agency, or community.

FOCUS OF REAL-TIME TRAINING

The team is the vehicle for carrying out this training/learning and passing on the lessons for success. The team demonstrates synergistic results in performance, raising the bar with each result. The team possesses and shares more knowledge than any group of individuals and keeps up-to-date with rapid changes. The team shares successes and failures, showing a tirelessness in performance by relieving individuals who need to recoup their individual energy for performance. Sound too idealistic? The team does this only with continuous real-time learning about their own relationships, growth, performance, and results. The team does this with open and shared leadership— open to new ideas and shared among those who have the passion to move on with things.

The skeptics might ask, "But aren't teams old hat by now?" The answer is, "Yes, but so what?" If teams did not show value in their performance, they would have perished from their own weight. The fact that teams have been around for a long time is evidence that they contribute to the success of organizations, communities, businesses, and agencies. Another answer is that intense interest in teams continues due to individuals' positive experiences with teams from the past.

Consider this example. At the beginning of a four-day simulation designed to enhance individual and team learning in the business setting, a participant voiced this expectation: "In college, I was a member of the crew team. When we all pulled on those oars with exactly the same force at precisely the same time, that shell literally leapt out of the water. The feeling was euphoric. I've been trying to re-create that feeling in my work setting for over twenty years. I hope to get the experience here to be able to accomplish that goal."

LESSONS OF SUCCESS

The reason this person wanted to re-create the feeling is self-evident. The euphoric feeling comes from incredible team success at task accomplishment. The result for the organization is not just an individual who feels good. The result is success for the organization as well. Training for the skills a team needs to succeed at task accomplishment is imperative. There is both complexity and simplicity in learning the skills necessary to re-create such results and the feeling of euphoria that comes from them.

The first learning must be about open and shared leadership. How does one learn to lead? Leadership can be described as a position, a set of traits, or a process. It requires vision, clear goals, measurable standards, and many other attributes. All of these viewpoints have some validity. However, in both the simplest and most encompassing points of view, leadership is activity.

LEADERSHIP AS ACTIVITY

Leadership is an activity that takes place between one person and others. The quality of leadership is determined by whether the "leader" is followed by others. Followership happens when a leader exercises influence and achieves the desired result. Therefore, it is self-evident that a leader must learn the skill to influence. This is the first complexity. How do you train someone in how to influence?

Leadership (read influence) happens within a context. That is, there are three elements present in any leadership situation: the leader, those to be influenced, and the environment within which the attempt takes place. These three variables are never constant. Literally everything matters. Procedures that worked well in one situation may not help at all in a slightly different one. In addition, phrases such as, "I feel really great" or "This is a bad hair day" are examples of how individual attitudes and openness to influence may change from one day or even one moment to the next. But there is a second complexity. How do you train people to adjust for a constantly changing context?

Leadership in this environment must be open and shared. Open because in a changing environment there is no one rule of behavior that always gets the same results. Shared because in a world of increasing information no one person can know everything required to achieve success. Given these challenges, what is the requirement for training? Or can training even solve the problem and meet the demand?

BECOMING A LEARNING TEAM

The current answer to the dilemma above is to become a learning team. That is, all team members must keep the learning hat on and adjust behaviors based on the differences confronted. This means that training must happen continually, not just in the classroom, but in real time—learning and reflecting with the help of a trainer (facilitator). The skills for continuous real-time learning are fairly straightforward and can be taught. However, proficiency in the skills comes only with real-time practice in organizational settings.

Practicing the skills demands that the team members develop mutually agreeable methods to communicate feelings of confusion, joy, perceived inconsistencies between practice and vision or values, or other distractors that may impede mission success.

The problem in performing this continuous real-time learning results from the experience each of us has with the concept of "learning." A mental image of a classroom with a favorite or difficult teacher from our past springs to mind. Most positively, we may think, "There's a lesson to be learned and this teacher will help me see what it is. Once I know the lesson, I can apply it whenever it's useful." However, the complexity of a continually changing context means that this early definition of learning does not apply. There is no one rule the teacher will tell us. We must discover the best means to proceed by continuous learning within the context of the team and the situation at hand.

THE ROLE OF CONTINUOUS LEARNING

Does continuous learning mean that learning never ends? A participant in a team learning simulation expressed this concern: "This is the third management-development program I've participated in. I know about teaming." Is that true? The answer is unquestionably yes. Will the participant be successful in this setting? The answer is, "It depends." It depends on the skill of reading the demands of a new setting and adjusting skills to the new situation. Because there is no one single rule of behavior to follow, the individual must read the situation before acting. Success will be determined by demonstration of respect for the other team members, by how willing the other members are to show the same respect and to be influenced, by how willing they all are to both give and receive feedback on their individual and collective actions, and the situation this particular team collectively faces. Elements affecting success also include such factors as time pressures, the likelihood of success given other environmental considerations, and how accepting the larger organization will be of the team's outcomes.

So, if our past experience of learning does not apply, what is the new model for team learning? Team learning is based on the notion that teams take time to develop and trust one another. As the team "matures," both trust and empowerment increase. However, the team development model is not a linear one. With each change in membership, every time lag in teamwork, or changing demands and problems, the team must re-confront issues of team performance. This is what makes team learning continuous.

A Model for Team Learning

Continuous team learning requires four behaviors that take place within each team activity. Although the theory can be "trained," the application must be practiced by continuous learning and reflection every time the team meets. As shown in Figure 1, team members learn by doing the following:

- Investing time,
- Managing differences,
- Gaining full participation, and
- Achieving results.

In fact, one might say that the training/learning comes from doing the first three steps, and then achieving results takes care of itself.

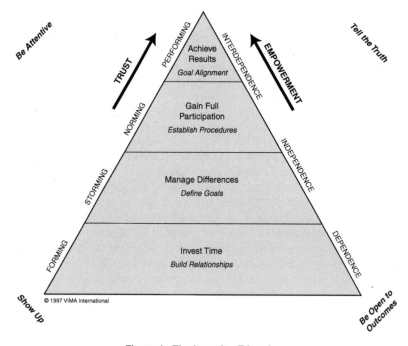

Figure 1. The Learning Triangle

The model of team learning shown in Figure 1 may also explain why conventional classroom training models are an anachronism. Many training programs focus on skills such as managing differences or gaining full participation. Unfortunately, few of these programs sufficiently emphasize the first requirement, investing time. It is during the investment of time, sometimes to the detriment of other obligations, that teams develop, that reflection happens, and that learning occurs. Simply put, training takes time—not in the classroom—but as a part of every team activity.

If this is not training in the classical sense, then who does the training? Who is the translator, tour guide, or facilitator? Some organizations have the luxury of providing a person trained in facilitation. The facilitator requires the team to take time away from its task focus to ask itself the questions about how they are doing. This is where the learning takes place. However, even when an external facilitator is present, learning is still the responsibility of each team member. If the team is to be successful in learning and continuing to meet mission success with euphoria, it demands the constant vigilance of each team member to the four tenets of the new learning model: investing time, managing differences, gaining full participation, and achieving results. Training and learning must be done by the members themselves.

CONTINUOUS TEAM LEARNING

How can a team start the process of continuous training/learning? Surely there are enough demands on time that it will not be easy to invest more in a continuous learning process that demands frequent interpersonal communication. Communication about team performance can be made easier by using a feedback instrument, usually in the form of a questionnaire, in order to generate hard-to-get-at process data and thereby deepen the lessons learned. The feedback instrument should demonstrate variance in member responses to questions that produce useful data to open conversation. For example, if one person answers "rarely" when others answer "usually" to some particular behavior, a dialogue will be created among team members. This communication provides an opportunity for team learning to occur.

Feedback instruments that elicit perceived performance on the four principles that follow will enable the team members, the leader, and the group as a whole to assess their own strengths and weaknesses in any of the team learning processes:

- Investing time,

- Managing differences,

- Gaining full participation, and

- Achieving results.

Flowing from these principles are several behavioral imperatives that provide the individual actions one must perform to achieve the principle fully. For example, if one is to invest time, what must one do? What behaviors demonstrate that the member is investing time in the success of the team?

A sample of survey questions that assess a team's performance in the four stages of investing time, gaining participation, managing differences, and achieving results is given in Figure 2. The *Light Bulbs for Leaders: Team Assessment Survey* (VIMA International, 1997) includes the assessment, interpretation, and action planning guidelines for teams to develop throughout these four stages.

Feedback from the instrument is gathered in the form of both numerical responses and narrative comments addressing the greatest team problems. Comments also address what should be continued, started, and stopped for maximum team effectiveness, leader effectiveness, and individual member effectiveness. Data from objective assessment instruments is useful only to the degree that it creates dialogue among team members. The questionnaire results themselves do not necessarily provide the blueprint for team learning. They only provide the agenda for discussion that allows the team to take responsibility for and to begin their own team learning procedures.

LEARNING FROM DIALOGUE AND REFLECTION

The dialogue based on the instrument is real-time learning and allows the facilitator to guide team members in their own individual learning. Learning may apply to the particular team, the organizational setting, or the particular challenge. Learning takes place continuously as the team hones its skills, increases its performance, and experiences the euphoria of a well-oiled system. At each stage of development, reflection must continue as the team members become more proficient at using the skills of team learning to improve performance.

Can this real-time learning take place in a classroom? Probably not. Tools that enable the team learning process to take place can be demonstrated in the classroom, but the payoff is in the real-time learning on the job. So,

TEAM ASSESSMENT SURVEY

Part 1

Instructions: Using the six-point scale below, indicate your level of agreement with each of the statements listed. Your responses should be based on your work team's actual behavior.

1	2	3	4	5	6
Strongly Disagree	Disagree	Slightly Disagree	Slightly Agree	Agree	Strongly Agree

Response

1. Team members make an effort to learn one another's talents and abilities. _____

2. Team members allow time at each meeting to get reacquainted, revisit ideas, and prepare to move forward. _____

3. Roles and responsibilities are clarified and agreed to by team members. _____

4. Team members build on one another's ideas. _____

5. Leadership shifts from member to member, depending on the circumstances and topic. _____

6. Desired outcomes are regularly achieved and used as a measure of the team's success. _____

7. Team members openly share perspectives and discuss differences. _____

8. The team outcomes foster achievement of the organization's goals. _____

Figure 2. Team Assessment Survey Sample

Part 2

Think about the ways in which you and your colleagues work to meet your mission. In your opinion, what does your team need to do to foster a climate of teamwork? Please be specific in describing behaviors the team could use when working together.

To foster teamwork, the team needs to **Continue Doing:**

_____

_____

_____

_____

_____

_____

_____

To foster teamwork, the team needs to **Start Doing:**

_____

_____

_____

_____

_____

_____

_____

To foster teamwork, the team needs to **Stop Doing:**

_____

_____

_____

_____

_____

_____

_____

Figure 2. Team Assessment Survey Sample (continued)

back to work for all the teams, with one caveat. Where training is concerned, enough is never enough! Learning (read training) must occur continuously with every team challenge. Training is constant and team members themselves must be their own trainers, learning on their own.

Reference

Robert, E.A., & Glacel, B.P. (1996). *Light bulbs for leaders: A guide book for team learning*. New York: John Wiley.

Emile A. Robert, Jr., Ph.D., *is COO of VIMA International, Inc.—The Leadership Group. He has over thirty years' experience in human resource development and administration. He is an acknowledged authority in organization development, personnel assessment and evaluation, forecasting human resource needs, and professional development. Dr. Robert works with clients across the United States as well as in Scotland, New Zealand, Southeast Asia, and South Africa. He is on the adjunct faculty at the Center for Creative Leadership and the co-author of* Light Bulbs for Learning: A Guide Book for Team Learning.

Barbara Pate Glacel, Ph.D., *is CEO of VIMA International, Inc.—The Leadership Group. Dr. Glacel consults in executive and organizational development for organizations such as Lockheed Martin Corporation, the MITRE Corporation, NASA, MCI, and the Atlantic Richfield Corporation, as well as other organizations in Europe, Africa, and the Pacific Rim. She has served as vice president of the Instructional Systems Association, vice president of the Alumni Board of Directors of the College of William and Mary, adjunct faculty member at the Center for Creative Leadership, and policy advisor to the Secretary of the Army and the Secretary of Defense. She is the co-author of* Light Bulbs for Leaders: A Guide Book for Team Learning.

MANAGING TIME IN CLASS

Scott B. Parry

Abstract: Trainers are managers. We manage people: trainees, other presenters, AV support staff, etc. We manage resources: facilities, equipment, food services, and so on. And we manage time: start, finish, breaks, and staying on schedule. This article focuses on time management in the training room. It presents some factors that make management of classroom time difficult and gives practical methods a trainer can use to manage time successfully.

WHY TIME MANAGEMENT BECOMES AN ISSUE

Course developers put time estimates on each activity and exercise, but these are merely meant as guidelines. Different sessions require different amounts of time to reach the objectives of a given learning activity. Yet the length of the course is usually fixed and cannot be expanded to accommodate a group that is slower, more verbal, or fascinated by the subject.

To the degree that enrollment in a session is controlled or limited to those who have the need and the prerequisites (experience, knowledge, etc.) the group will be easier to manage. A homogeneous group is much easier to manage and keep on schedule than a heterogeneous group. Additionally, each time we teach a course, our repertoire of anecdotes, examples, and experiences gleaned from participants grows larger. Each offering of a training program is likely to be richer than those that preceded it. Add to this the tendency of sponsors or clients to think of new subjects that should be included in the training—new content to be "worked in" the next time we run the course.

In summary, the following four factors make the management of classroom time extremely difficult:

- The difference in learning time required from group to group and from individual to individual;

- The degree to which participants constitute a homogeneous or a heterogeneous group;

- The expanding repertoire of the instructor that becomes richer each time a course is taught; and

- The tendency to add new topics to a course without deleting or shortening existing material.

Consider this situation. You are midway through a course you have taught several times. Yet this group is less experienced than past ones, and you are two hours behind where you should be. What should you do?

(a) Tell participants, "We'll have to step up the pace, cut down on the questions, and eliminate some of the 'hands-on' exercises in order to cover everything and still get out on time."

(b) Study the remaining schedule during a break and decide which of your presentations can be eliminated or shortened without losing the practice sessions ("hands-on" applications) and without extending the length of the course.

Before reading further, decide which option you would pursue.

The tradeoff here is one of content versus process. Option A focuses on content: It is important to cover everything, even at the expense of comprehension and retention. Option B focuses on process: It is important that participants achieve mastery of what we do cover, even if this means jettisoning some of the content. Which is better? That depends (a diplomatic and safe answer, albeit less than satisfying)!

If you are teaching personnel policy, EEO, OSHA compliance, or some other topic that is heavy on information, documented in handouts or manuals, and your main objective (sometimes legalistic) is to make sure that participants were exposed to the policy and rules, then Option A might make more sense.

If you are teaching skills (supervisory, selling, data entry, assembly, troubleshooting) and your main objective is to develop new habits and improve performance, and if it is essential that your participants achieve mastery of the key skills and techniques, even at the expense of less important ones, then Option B might make more sense.

Here we arrive at the crux of the time-management dilemma: How you manage your time in a course, as in life, depends on your objectives and priorities. Your decision to retain or to jettison a given activity should be based primarily on the degree to which it moves your participants toward the attainment of the key learning objectives. Whether it is fun; whether they love it; whether it is one of your favorites—all these are secondary considerations. Sorry about that.

There is a tendency among inexperienced instructors to worry about having enough to say and enough material to fill the allotted time. Seasoned trainers know that participative instruction often takes more time than indicated on the schedule or lesson plan. Their concern is with letting participants out on time.

TIME-MANAGEMENT GUIDELINES FOR THE TRAINER

The guidelines that follow should help you in fulfilling your responsibility for managing time in class:

1. The time estimates for activities in training manuals are usually expressed in minutes and not in clock time (authors of training manuals do not know when you plan to start each day). Enter the expected clock times in the margin beside each activity so that you can see at a glance throughout the day whether you are running ahead or behind schedule.

2. You may also want to record your actual time spent on each activity (or your actual clock time at various points). This might be helpful the next time you administer the program. You will know when to modify the pace.

3. Do not worry if the group takes *less* time than you anticipated to read a handout, make a report, et cetera. Rather than filling the allotted time (which may slow the pace and cause the day to drag), move on to the next activity. You may be grateful for the extra time later in the day when you need it for another learning activity. (No instructor ever received bad reviews for letting a class out early!)

4. You are expected to make tradeoffs from one activity to another—to rob Peter to pay Paul. When courses are developed, the flow of instruction (learning sequences) comes from a "master plan" in the mind of the course designer. There was a logic to it, but participants are not privy to this logic. They ask questions and introduce information out of sequence. Thus, effective time management means knowing the content and purpose of each activity. If these are covered earlier, then on a subsequent activity you may find that you need less time than the course designer estimated. Conversely, if the content is not being fully covered or the purposes are not being met, you might conclude that the group is not ready yet and wait until a later activity. Make note of this in the margin of your instructor guidelines.

5. When participants raise issues that you will be discussing later in the course and that cannot be answered in a minute or two, you may want to start a follow-up list. Take a sheet of flip-chart paper, tape it to the wall, and label it "follow up" or "hanging issues." Then each time a participant raises a question or topic that can better be addressed later, make a note of it. Add the participant's name (and a note on your lesson plan, indicating where you will bring it up). Incidentally, this sheet is also a great place to put questions you do not know answers to or topics that are political "hot potatoes" that you want to clear with someone before addressing. The list buys you time to do your homework.

6. Sometimes participants have their own agendas and will raise issues that do not relate to the purpose of your class. Their psychological needs do

not always mesh with your logical or chronological needs! What can you do? Here are several ways of dealing with the participant who raises an irrelevant issue:

- If it can be addressed and dismissed in a minute or two, handle it. This is easier than making a scene.

- Ask the participant how the issue relates to the objectives of the activity or class (which you have made known in advance).

- Explain that the issue is one you would like to address but that you cannot take the time to do it justice during class. Ask the person to see you during a break or at lunch, along with anyone else who might be interested.

- If the same individuals continue to bring up irrelevant or personal issues, talk to them during a break or after class.

7. If you are running behind schedule, you can use subgroups to pick up the pace. A discussion will usually reach a conclusion much more quickly in a subgroup of two to four people than it will in a large group.

8. Similarly, by using subgroups for a division of labor, you can speed up an activity. For example, suppose the group has just read a four-page handout followed by six questions you were going to discuss in full session, but the group took longer to read the handout than other groups have taken. Break them into three subgroups and give two different questions to each, to discuss for two minutes and report on for a minute. Total time: 5 minutes, compared to 10 or 15 minutes in full session.

9. On activities for which a flip chart is being used to record ideas and responses from participants, save time by pre-lettering headings on each sheet prior to class and by appointing a recorder to write the entries during class. You cannot lead discussion and write simultaneously, and much time is lost with everyone waiting while you record a point before going on to the next point. The recorder will have more time than you to print or write neatly and spell correctly.

10. Similarly, use participants to distribute handouts, collect assignments, go make copies, turn on the projector, turn off lights, and so on. You can thus be instructing the group while these administrative chores are being handled.

11. The model you set for punctuality will determine the group's behavior in starting on time and in returning from breaks and lunch at the designated times. The session should also end at the scheduled time. If you do have to run over (make this an exception rather than the rule), negotiate this with the group and do not assume they are a captive audience.

12. Participants will work faster, the pace will move better, and breaks will be shorter if there are refreshments in or near the classroom. The same holds true for the proximity of phones, rest rooms, eating facilities, and so on. Of course, you may have little, if any, control over the facilities.

13. When you want to break into subgroups, instead of sending participants to breakout rooms and losing five minutes each way, have the subgroups work in different locations in the main room or select a seating arrangement in which participants can sit in subgroups at individual tables that are facing the front of the room.

14. When you break the participants into subgroups, give them a time limit and have each subgroup appoint a timekeeper to make sure they stay on target and are ready to reconvene on time.

15. Use a wrist watch or alarm clock that has a soft buzzer. At the start of longer activities, set it to go off 5 minutes before the end of the time period. This is your reminder to begin to wrap up. If participants are working in subgroups, you may also wish to say, "You have 5 minutes left."

16. Have the participants elect a time manager. Equip this person with two hand-held signs (about the size of Ping-Pong® paddles). One sign is an octagonal red STOP sign, which the time manager can hold up 2 or 3 minutes before the indicated end time of each topic or session (especially if you have not begun your wrap up). The other sign is a triangular YIELD sign, which is used to call your attention to someone who has a hand up and should be recognized. (It helps to seat the manager where the entire class is in view.) These signs are a graphic way to let the group know that time management is a shared responsibility.

The suggestions presented above can make managing time in the workshop or seminar room much easier for trainers.

Scott B. Parry is a psychologist, consultant, trainer, and chairman of Training House, Inc., creators of instructional programs and assessments. His Managerial Assessment of Proficiency (MAP) has been translated into five languages. He has published numerous articles and is the author of four books and dozens of published training courses. He has conducted more than four hundred "Train the Trainer" workshops and has addressed HRD conferences in several dozen countries.

THE SHIFT FROM TRAINING TO PERFORMANCE

Dana Gaines Robinson and James C. Robinson

Abstract: To quote a phrase from one of Bob Dylan's songs, the times are a-changin'. No statement better acknowledges the transformations occurring within the human resource development (HRD) profession. The profession is considered to be over fifty years old, but there has been little change in the method of delivery until now. For the most part, HRD professionals have been employed for the design and delivery of training curricula to enhance skills and knowledge. This paper addresses the changes the HRD profession is facing and looks at the future of the profession.

This article was excerpted from the book *Moving from Training to Performance: A Practical Guidebook,* Dana Gaines Robinson and James C. Robinson (Eds.). © 1998. Berrett-Koehler and the American Society for Training and Development. Used with permission.

A recent survey of more than three hundred senior and executive-level HRD professionals (ASTD, 1998) identified the ten most probable trends in the profession—both now and in three years' time. The "shift from providing training to improving performance" was ranked as the third most probable trend today and over the next three years. It appears that the mission of the profession is changing from providing skills and knowledge to the improvement of human performance on the job. This trend raises questions for both individuals and for the functions in which they work. How does one make the transition from operating as a training department to working as a performance-management and performance-improvement function?

CHANGES THAT ARE OCCURING

The training profession is undergoing the most dramatic changes since training was formally established as a profession in the 1940s. The HRD profession is transforming itself in several ways.

Downsizing

HRD departments are downsizing. In *Rethinking Human Resources: A Research Report,* published by the Conference Board in 1995, 58 percent of large U.S. corporations reported that they had downsized their HRD departments. In many cases, the staff had decreased by as much as 50 percent.

Outsourcing

Traditional HR jobs are increasingly being outsourced. The American Society for Training and Development's (ASTD) Benchmarking Forum (1995), a consortium of fifty organizations, reports that contract workers comprise 23 percent of their training design and development staff and 30 percent of their instructors. Sixty-six percent of people who responded to a 1996 Fax Forum in *Training & Development* expect to be external providers in ten years' time. Now entire training departments are outsourced to a provider. For example, DuPont's training function is entirely staffed by Forum Corporation employees.

Alternative Delivery

Alternatives to leader-led training are growing. Currently, almost 31 percent of structured learning is delivered by a means other than leader-led; most of this training is through multimedia.

New Positions

There is also an increase in demand for specialized positions such as performance technologists, performance consultants, and interactive learning specialists, replacing the traditional generic "trainer." In addition, traditional "training" departments may now be called "performance" departments.

WHY THESE CHANGES ARE OCCURING

A combination of forces is converging to create a new environment in which the training profession must operate. Some of these forces result from a growing dissatisfaction with traditional training results: (1) the cost of training continues to rise, yet less than 30 percent of what people learn is ever actually used on the job; (2) many training functions do not focus on results; and (3) there seem to be ambivalent relationships between many training departments and management.

A second set of forces arises from the opportunities presented by new business realities, including (1) globalization of businesses; (2) the escalating and constantly changing skill needs of employees; and (3) the opportunities that technology offers, both for skills that must be learned and as new means to deliver learning.

The question we might ask is whether the current focus on performance is simply a fad. We offer a resounding "No!" The current focus is based on the discipline of human performance technology that dates back to the 1950s. Human performance technology is defined as "the science of improving human performance in the workplace through analysis and the design, solution, and implementation of appropriate interventions" (Robinson & Robinson, 1998).

Although the focus on performance is not new, it has become more accentuated due to two contemporary business requirements: (1) a need to partner with management and (2) a need to link human performance requirements with business needs.

Today's business world requires that training functions work in partnership with management. The focus on performance improvement requires that significant resources be allocated to forming and sustaining these partnerships. Because the individuals within the management group with whom these partnerships are formed are referred to as "clients," the term "performance consultant" was coined to describe the "trainer's" role.

Today's business world also requires that human resource development be linked to business needs. After the business goal is defined, a performance department works with clients to answer the question, "What must people do more, better, or differently if this business goal is to be achieved?" This ensures that the performance requirements are linked to business and operational goals. It also ensures that the performance department will be more strategic and proactive.

Never has there been a greater opportunity for training departments to partner with management to achieve exceptional performance and business results. However, there is a great deal of work associated with a transformation from a training department into a performance department. It will not occur just because the department gives itself a new name. The transition process typically requires between two and four years.

CHARACTERISTICS OF A PERFORMANCE FOCUS

Most HRD departments are focused somewhere between the traditional "training" focus of the past and the "performance" focus described here. The following characteristics provide an idea of the unique characteristics of a performance department.

People in the Department

- Focus on what people need to do with what they learn, not on the acquisition of skill or knowledge. Training is seen as a means to the ultimate goal of enhancing performance.

- Are process-oriented, as opposed to event-oriented.

- Initiate opportunities to work in a proactive manner.

- Approach situations in a manner that is bias-free regarding solutions (rather than assuming that training is required).

- Must be partnered to a client (the "owner" of the business process to which the project is linked).

- View front-end assessment as mandatory, including identification of barriers in the work environment that inhibit desired performance.
- Measure success in terms of impact on performance and on the operation.

The ultimate work of a performance department is to define and align four types of needs: business needs, performance needs, learning needs, and work environment needs.

Business needs are the goals for a unit, department, or organization, usually expressed in operational or numeric terms, for example, a business goal could be to increase customer satisfaction. *Performance needs* are on-the-job requirements describing what people must do if the business needs are to be achieved; they usually are measured in behavioral terms. *Learning needs* define the skills and knowledge that people must have in order to perform successfully. *Work environment needs* identify the systems and processes that surround performers in their job environments.

WHAT THE FUTURE HOLDS

Now is one of the most exhilarating and challenging times to be involved in the HRD field. So much change is taking place. What worked before is no longer effective, so new processes and roles are being created. The services provided before are no longer sufficient, so new services and jobs are being developed. Although the most obvious change is the new focus on performance improvement, other innovative shifts will surely occur. We predict the following:

An Integrated Structure. In the future, the human resource, training, and organization development functions will utilize a shared process and form an integrated structure. This will occur because it is more efficient and prevents the typical silo structure from occurring. It is likely that the performance department of the future will have both a strategic unit and a tactical unit.

Centralized Work Process with Decentralized Operations. The work process will be centralized, while those who support the process will be decentralized. Although there continues to be a debate over whether the training and HR functions should be centralized or decentralized, we believe the focus on performance makes the answer obvious. The human performance improvement process must be centralized, with some systems in place to ensure that it is being utilized in a quality manner and as intended by all those working within it. However, the employees within the performance department will be dispersed both functionally and geographically. It is highly probable that performance consultants and performance analysts, the people responsible for the strategic side of the business, will be located at the same sites as their client groups. These individuals will make it possible for clients to make comprehensive requests of the HRD department, as all requests to shape human performance in support of business goals will flow through these consultants and analysts.

The tactical specialists, however, are likely to form a shared services group, housed in a central location. For example, instructional designers and compensation specialists can be based at a corporate location. The trend to outsource these services will continue, and these tactical specialists will in all likelihood present the greatest opportunity for using external services.

Position of Performance Consultant. The position of performance consultant will become the norm in organizations. Although the job may not always be referred to by this title, the demand for people to fill this type of position is escalating rapidly. These people are on the front line, helping clients to translate their business goals into human performance requirements. As clients have begun to realize the benefits of such a position, the demand has grown. It is safe to say that performance consulting is a growth industry!

Line Managers As Full Performance Partners. Performance language will be known and used by line managers as they become full partners in trying to achieve performance goals. At some point in the near future, clients will recognize the value in thinking and talking performance. They will be able to describe a need for service in performance, not solution, language. They will expect and want some level of assessment to occur prior to implementing a solution. They will acknowledge the probability that *multiple* interventions, not a single intervention, will be required in order to change performance.

This change will be one of the primary benefits derived from the strong relationships forged between performance consultants and their clients. Through those relationships, learning and development will occur in two ways: (1) the performance consultant will learn about the business of the business, and (2) the client will learn about human performance technology and how to enhance performance in support of business goals. In essence, the technology will be transferred so that each client becomes a performance partner for his or her own performance and area of responsibility.

Although no one can ever be certain of the future, enough signs exist in organizations to suggest that these changes are likely to occur in the near future. Our profession is immersed in a major transformation. Those of us who work in it must transform as well. Although the challenges are many, there will also be many rewards.

References

ASTD. (1995) *Benchmarking forum*. Alexandria, VA: Author.

ASTD. (1996, April) Fax forum. *Training and Development*, p.13.

ASTD. (1997) *Trends in HRD*. Alexandria, VA: Author.

Csoka, L. (1995). *Rethinking human resources*. New York: The Conference Board.

Robinson, D.G., & Robinson, J.C. (1998). *Moving from training to performance: A practical guidebook*. Alexandria, VA: ASTD and San Francisco, CA: Berrett-Koehler.

Dana Gaines Robinson, B.A., M.Ed., is president of Partners in Change, Inc. She is a recognized leader in the areas of performance technology and impact measurement. Ms. Robinson assists HR and HRD functions to transition from a traditional focus on training per se to one that focuses on performance improvement. She is a frequent speaker at national conferences, including the American Society for Training and Development, Training, and AME/Linkage, Inc. With Jim Robinson, Dana co-authored Training for Impact: How to Link Training to Business Needs *and* Measure the Results and Performance Consulting: Moving Beyond Training. *They also co-edited* Moving from Training to Performance: A Practical Guidebook.

James C. Robinson, M.S., M.A., is chairman of Partners in Change, Inc. He is a recognized leader in the areas of human resource development and performance consulting. Mr. Robinson helps organizations to develop performance models and competency models to improve employee performance and capability. He is a frequent speaker at national conferences, including the American Society for Training and Development and the International Society for Performance Improvement (ISPI). With Dana Robinson, he has co-authored Training for Impact: How to Link Training to Business Needs *and* Measure the Results and Performance Consulting: Moving Beyond Training. *They also co-edited* Moving from Training to Performance: A Practical Guidebook.

HOW TO DESIGN AND GUIDE DEBRIEFING

Sivasailam "Thiagi" Thiagarajan

Abstract: Debriefing is the process of facilitating discussion to help participants reflect on their experiences during an experiential activity, gain valuable
insights, and share them with one another. The design of a debriefing is as important as the design of
the activity itself. This article describes a three-step
process for the systematic design and flexible use of
a debriefing guide.

The first step in the process involves analyzing the
experiential activity and generating seven lists cover-
ing *events, adjectives, objects, feelings, people, principles,*
and *scenarios.* These lists form the basis for preparing
debriefing questions dealing with six topics: "How do
you feel?" "What happened?" "What did you learn?"
"How does this relate?" "What if?" and "What next?"
During the actual debriefing session, these sets of
questions are used in a flexible fashion.

A fundamental truth in experiential learning is that participants do not automatically learn from experience. They learn from reflecting on the experience, gaining valuable insights, and sharing these insights with one another. *Debriefing* is the process that facilitates this type of reflection and discussion.

Designing a debriefing is as important as designing the experiential activity itself. Based on thirty years' of experience debriefing experiential activities, I have developed the three-step approach described below:

1. Analyze the experiential activity and prepare seven lists of points related to it.
2. Construct six sets of debriefing questions.
3. Use the debriefing questions in a flexible fashion.

PREPARE SEVEN LISTS OF POINTS ABOUT THE ACTIVITY

First analyze the experiential activity, looking for the following:

- Events and decision points within the activity,
- Adjectives that describe different events and outcomes of the activity,
- Objects and artifacts used in the activity,
- Feelings that are likely to be aroused by the activity,
- People involved in the activity,
- Principles brought out by the activity, and
- Scenarios brought to mind by variations on the activity.

To fill in the basic information for these lists, carefully review the activity, participant materials, and the facilitator guide. Walk through the activity and note its critical aspects. Collect additional information by pilot testing the activity with representative participants. Some specific guidelines for each of the seven lists are given below:

List of Events

- Prepare an outline of the major events during the experiential activity.

- Prepare a list of major decision points within the activity.

List of Adjectives

- Prepare a list of words and phrases that describe different aspects of the experiential activity.

- Add a set of standard adjectives such as "important," "surprising," "painful," "frustrating, or "practical."

- Use the list of events you developed earlier to identify additional adjectives.

- Incorporate adjectives suggested by participants during subsequent debriefing sessions.

List of Objects

- Prepare a list of objects used during the activity.

- Use the list of events you developed earlier to identify additional objects.

- Classify the objects into different categories, for example, an actual object, such as a corporate form, or a substitute object, such as a pen that represents a company product.

List of Feelings

- Prepare a list of words and phrases that describe feelings likely to be aroused by the activity.

- Select suitable words from the Thesaurus of Feeling Terms in Figure 1.

- Use a master set of feeling words based on your previous experiences with similar activities.

- Incorporate additional words suggested by participants during subsequent debriefing sessions.

List of People

- Prepare a list of different roles assigned to participants during the activity.

- Add different types of participants (such as men and women, analytical and impulsive personalities) that may respond differently to the activity.

- Use the list of events you developed earlier to identify additional groupings of participants.

adventurous	encouraged	negative	smart
afraid	energetic	nervous	sneaky
aggressive	engaged	nice	sorry
agitated	enthusiastic	obtuse	spiteful
alarmed	exasperated	optimistic	startled
alert	excited	ordinary	stimulated
alone	exhausted	paranoid	strange
amazed	exhilarated	passive	strong
ambivalent	flexible	peaceful	stubborn
amused	flustered	persecuted	stuck
angry	foolish	pessimistic	stunned
annoyed	fragile	playful	stupid
anxious	framed	pleased	subdued
ashamed	frantic	positive	successful
betrayed	free	powerful	surprised
bored	frustrated	powerless	suspicious
calm	glad	pressured	sympathetic
challenged	grateful	productive	tense
cheated	greedy	proud	tentative
comfortable	guarded	provoked	terrible
competitive	guilty	puzzled	thankful
confident	happy	quarrelsome	third-rate
confrontational	helpless	refreshed	threatened
confused	hesitant	regretful	thrilled
cooperative	hopeless	rejected	thwarted
curious	hostile	relaxed	tired
defeated	humiliated	relieved	touched
defensive	hurt	reluctant	touchy
delighted	ignorant	remorseful	trapped
depressed	ignored	resentful	tricked
desperate	impatient	rewarded	troubled
detached	incompetent	righteous	trusting
determined	indecisive	rigid	uncertain
different	indifferent	sad	uncomfortable
diffident	inept	sarcastic	uneasy
disappointed	insecure	satisfied	unfair
discouraged	inspired	scared	unsure
disillusioned	insulted	secure	upset
disinterested	intimidated	self-conscious	uptight
distracted	intrigued	set up	useless
dominated	involved	settled	vulnerable
eager	isolated	shallow	wary
effective	jumpy	shocked	weak
embarrassed	lost	silly	withdrawn
empty	mean	skeptical	worried
enchanted	miserable	slow	wretched

Figure 1. Thesaurus of Feeling Terms

List of Principles

- Prepare a list of principles by analyzing the issues that are introduced in the activity.
- Use the list of events you developed to identify additional principles.
- Use the list of feelings you created earlier to formulate additional principles linking participant behaviors with specific feelings.
- Add additional principles suggested by subject-matter experts.
- Incorporate additional principles suggested by participants during subsequent debriefing sessions.

List of Scenarios

- Prepare a list of several "What if?" questions related to the activity.
- Use the list of events you created earlier to suggest additional scenarios.
- Use a standard set of "What if?" questions that speculate about variations in time, number of participants, and scoring procedures.
- Use the list of objects you developed to suggest additional scenarios involving different objects.
- Incorporate additional scenarios suggested by the participants during subsequent debriefing sessions.

PREPARE SIX LISTS OF DEBRIEFING QUESTIONS

The seven lists prepared in the preceding step form the basis for constructing the following six general debriefing questions:

- How do you feel?
- What happened?
- What did you learn?
- How does it relate to your work or personal life?
- What if?
- What next?

As Figure 2 shows, the relationship between the seven lists and the six questions is not direct. Instead, each set of questions may be based on more than one list. In general, each set begins with a broad open-ended question. Encourage the participants to reflect back on their participation in the experiential activity before answering. Use specific questions after participants run out of comments and responses. Figure 2 shows how the debriefing questions link with the topics.

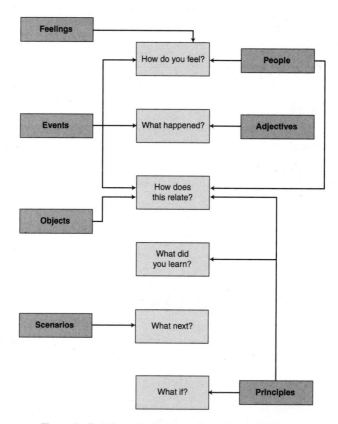

Figure 2. Relationship Between Questions and Topics

Specific suggestions for generating each of the six sets of questions are given below:

How Do You Feel?

This set of questions gives the participants an opportunity to express any strong emotions and clear the air. This venting process makes it easier for them to be more centered and objective during the later phases of debriefing.

Begin with a Broad Question. Invite the participants to get in touch with their feelings and emotions about the process and the outcomes of the experiential activity.

Explore Specific Classes of Feelings. Use the words and phrases from the list of feelings developed earlier. Ask the participants whether they experienced similar feelings during the experiential activity.

Discuss Feelings Related to Specific Events. Use the items from the list of events developed earlier. Recall major decision points and milestones from the activity. Encourage participants to discuss how they felt at specific times.

Discuss Feelings About Different Groups of People. Use the items from the list of people. Identify specific groups of people or roles in the experiential activity. Ask participants how they felt toward each group. Also ask members of each group how they felt about members of the other groups—and about themselves.

What Happened?

This set of questions permits you to collect data from different participants about what happened during the activity. Their recollections make it possible for the participants to compare and contrast their perceptions and to derive general principles for use in the next phase of debriefing.

Begin with a Broad Question. Ask participants to recall important events during their participation in the experiential activity.

Ask Questions About Specific Events. Use items from the list of events. Identify each event and ask participants to recall significant things that happened during that event.

Ask Questions About Specific Types of Events. Use items from the list of adjectives. Ask participants to recall events from the activity that they associate with each adjective.

What Did You Learn?

This set of questions encourages the participants to test different hypotheses about the experiential activity. This makes it possible for the participants to discover the learning points and to apply them to their real-world situations.

Begin with a Broad Question. Invite participants to come up with general principles based on their experiences from the activity.

Encourage Discussion of Each Principle. Ask the participants to treat each principle as a hypothesis and to offer experiential evidence from the activity to support or reject it. Encourage an open dialogue and inquiry.

Present Your Principles. If the discussion among the participants becomes redundant or slow, check the list of principles generated during the previous step. Offer one or more principles that were not discussed previously. Ask the participants for relevant data from the experiential activity.

How Does This Relate?

This set of questions encourages a discussion of the relevance of the experiential activity to the participants' workplaces. Participants suggest and discuss analogies between what happened during the activity and what happens in their real worlds.

Begin with a Broad Question. Ask the participants to explain how the experiential activity reflects events in their workplaces. Suggest that the activity is a metaphor and ask participants to speculate on what real-world events it is a metaphor for.

Discuss Specific Events from the Activity. Use items from the list of events. Identify specific events from the activity and ask the participants to come up with similar experiences they have had in the workplace.

Discuss Specific Objects and Artifacts. Use items from the list of objects. Identify specific objects used in the activity and ask the participants to find their workplace counterparts.

Discuss Specific Groups and Roles. Use items from the list of people. Ask the participants to identify similar groups of people or roles in their workplace. Encourage a discussion of the similarity between people's behavior in the experiential activity and in the real world.

Discuss Specific Principles. Use items from the list of principles. Ask the participants to discuss how each principle is reflected in their workplace experiences.

What If?

"What if?" questions encourage the participants to apply their insights to new contexts. These questions involve alternative scenarios to extrapolate from the experiential activity.

Begin with a Broad Question. Invite the participants to come up with questions that suggest variations in the experiential activity.

Encourage Speculation. Ask participants to conjecture how their behavior would have changed under each new context. Encourage in-depth discussions and dialogue.

Present Your Scenarios. If participants are unable to come up with additional "what if?" questions, check the list of scenarios. Present one or more scenarios that were not speculated on previously. Ask the participants to discuss the potential impact of these on their behavior.

Relate to Real-World Situations. Invite the participants to identify relevant variables in their workplace and how these affect their behavior.

What Next?

This set of questions facilitates the action-planning phase. The questions encourage the participants to come up with improved strategies for use in the future.

Ask for Better Strategies That Could Have Been Used. Ask participants how they would change their strategies if they were to participate in the same experiential activity again. Encourage them to make use of everything they learned from their initial experience.

Encourage Additional Action Planning. Use the list of people. Ask participants how they would behave differently if their roles had been different in the experiential activity. Also use the list of events to discuss specific changes during each event.

Encourage Real-World Action Planning. Ask participants how their workplace behaviors might change as a result of the insights gained from their participation in the experiential activity.

Discuss Specific Principles. Use the list of principles generated during the previous step and during the earlier discussion. Ask participants how they would apply each principle to their workplace situations.

Use the Debriefing Questions Flexibly

You now have six sets of questions for use during the debriefing session. These questions are not meant to be used in a linear, mechanical fashion, but rather as a safety net beneath a free-floating dialogue. During the debriefing, encourage and exploit spontaneous comments and let the discussion follow its natural flow. Fall back on your prepared set of questions during long periods of silence or repetition.

Position the debriefing session carefully. Acknowledge that participants have several exciting thoughts to express. Suggest the use of a suitable structure to facilitate thoughtful reflection and useful sharing of insights. Obtain the participants' permission to impose such a structure.

List the following six phases of debriefing on a flip chart:

- Events and decision points in the activity,

- Adjectives that describe different events and outcomes of the activity,

- Objects and artifacts used in the activity,

- Feelings that are likely to be aroused by the activity,

- People involved in the activity,

- Principles incorporated in the activity, and

- Scenarios speculating on variations to the activity.

Briefly explain the purpose of each phase and the rationale for the sequence. Work through each phase of debriefing, always beginning with a broad, open-ended question. Reserve the more specific probing questions for later. During the discussion, encourage participants to make any comments they like, even if they relate to one of the earlier phases in the debriefing process. A final suggestion for improving your facilitation skills: Debrief your own debriefing process through self-assessment.

Sivasailam "Thiagi" Thiagarajan, Ph.D.*, is president of Workshops by Thiagi and one of the principals for Qube Learning. Dr. Thiagarajan has lived in three different countries and has consulted in twenty-five others. The author of thirty books and designer of more than two-hundred training games, simulations, and experiential activities, he writes a monthly newsletter,* Thiagi GameLetter, *published by Jossey-Bass/Pfeiffer.*

SEDUCE: An Effective Approach to Experiential Learning

Lori L. Silverman and Linda Ernst

Abstract: We all know the value of experiential learning. It is the basis for the *Annual.* Participants typically walk away with increased knowledge and skill
retention after an enjoyable classroom learning experience. Yet many workshop designers and instructors do not employ experiential learning to ensure
these outcomes.

The SEDUCE approach to discovery learning
creates an environment in which learners realize on
their own what they need to know and/or do differently. The approach is seductive in that it can
transform initial resistance into willing, even avid,
interest. Participants are induced to enjoy things
they may not have intended to enjoy. They are en-
ticed into heightened levels of personal discovery
which, in turn, creates the dissonance necessary to
facilitate individual change. The SEDUCE acronym
will help you more easily remember the steps to
ensure successful experiential learning.

THE SEDUCE APPROACH TO EXPERIENTIAL LEARNING

Figure 1 depicts the SEDUCE approach to discovery learning. The five steps—start-up, experience, debrief, unveil concepts, and execute—are undertaken in the order shown. If a step is skipped or is taken out of order, participants may not fully achieve the desired learning objectives.

Before starting, determine the learning objective(s) and select an appropriate learning experience. This may be as formal as a workshop or class or may be a few minutes of on-the-job coaching. It may be an activity, a teaching module, or a participant game. Following is a detailed explanation of each step in the model.

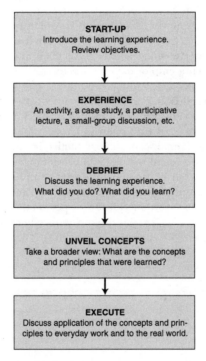

Figure 1. The SEDUCE Approach to Experiential Learning

Start-Up

The first step in the experiential learning process is the start-up. The purpose is to set up the learning experience. There are four ways to set up the experience. Use one or a combination of the following:

Purpose or Objective of the Activity. For an activity such as a participative lecture, begin by saying "What we're going to talk about today is . . . ." For a true experiential learning situation, such as a structured experience, the objective may be a part of what is discovered by the participants, so it would not be discussed at this point.

Explanation of What You Will Do. For a participative lecture, you may give information, show graphics, or ask and answer questions. In a small-group discussion, you may divide people into groups, give the assignment, and be available to coach and help groups as needed. Explain your role to the group.

What Participants Are Expected To Do. For a small-group discussion, the participants may be asked to discuss a situation, brainstorm ideas or solutions, and report to the group at large. During a video presentation, the participants may be asked to watch for key points, answer specific questions, or take notes for further discussion.

Rules That Accompany the Learning Experience. For an icebreaker the rules may be that participants should form groups of at least four members who have not previously met. For a technical lecture, the ground rules may include when to ask questions, for example, ask clarifying questions as they occur, but hold other questions until the end of the presentation.

Experience

The second step in the experiential learning process is the learning experience itself. The purpose of this step is to involve the participants actively in the learning experience. Types of learning experiences include the following:

- Case studies
- Computer-assisted learning
- Crossword puzzles
- Decision-making groups

- Demonstrations
- Discussions
- Giving and receiving feedback
- Hands-on experiences
- Participative lectures
- Practice sessions
- Questionnaires
- Role plays
- Self-study
- Session starters
- Small-group discussion
- Videotapes

The learning experience may be learner-directed or facilitator-directed. The more independent the learner and the more motivated to learn he or she is, the more learner-directed the experience can be. The novice learner may require more direction to facilitate learning.

Debrief

The third step in the experiential learning process is to debrief the learning experience. The purpose of the debrief is to help learners discover and share their reactions and experiences during the learning experience. The focus of the debrief is on the *content* of the learning experience. It is important that you not let the learners jump to concepts and learning principles too quickly.

If the learning experience was a structured experience, a game, or a participant activity, this step is meant to help the participants conclude the activity and get ready to move on to the learning points. This is a critical step, especially when an activity generates feelings, explores beliefs or values, or involves personal reactions. Some participants become involved in the topic or details of an activity and need time for discussion before they are ready to move to the next step.

It is most effective to use structured discussion as the instruction technique to facilitate debriefing a learning experience. To do this, explore what actually occurred during the activity, discuss issues specific to the content, and ask questions to generate reactions. In addition, there are several other instruction techniques that can help facilitate the debriefing discussion. You can (a) have each person write down his or her reactions or thoughts and then discuss them; (b) have small groups generate common reactions and then share them with the large group; or (c) have partners interview one another and report back to the large group.

Unveil Concepts

The fourth step in the experiential learning process is to unveil concepts. The purpose of this step is to help the learner identify and discuss the broader concepts and principles discovered during the learning experience. It is the "So what?" step. So, what was the point? So, what did we learn? So, what does it mean?

It is critical that the thoughts and ideas generated during this step come from the learners. If you reveal and explain the concepts and principles to the learners, they will still be your thoughts, "owned" by you rather then "discovered" by them. An inferential leap is necessary for the learners to move from the experience to learning about themselves or others.

If this step is omitted, the learning will be incomplete. Participants may later say that they enjoyed the activity, the lecture, or the discussion and may understand the specific issues of the learning experience, but be unable to report what they learned from it in broader terms. Some learners easily move from the specific to the conceptual; others will require prompting and coaching to discover broader concepts and principles.

Your role during this step is to guide the discussion so that it focuses on the learning points and moves away from the specific activity. In a discussion of a case study, for example, it is important that the discussion move to the concept taught by the case rather than stay with the details outlined in the story. After a participative lecture, ask questions of the learners to help them to summarize the main points and paraphrase key concepts.

This is the best time to chart answers, ideas, and concepts. It will help the learners remember the main points and will reinforce the concepts. Prompt the generation of concepts by asking, "What did you learn from this activity [discussion, practice session, case study] in general?" Ask about the general topic of the learning experience, for example, leadership, helping adults learn, managing time, or whatever. When listing concepts on a flip chart, avoid writing words or phrases that are specific to the activity. Help the participants move to a more general, conceptual level. For example, in the discussion of a case study in which unclear directions were an issue, rather than writing "Joe needed to give clearer directions," write "Give clear directions."

Execute ·

The final step in the experiential learning process is to "execute." This is the "Now what?" step. The purpose of this step is to help the learner identify what to do with the new information or skill. Without this step, some participants will be unable to apply the new learning in real-world situations. It will remain a theoretical, classroom idea. This step is the key to the entire learning experience.

Your role in this step, as in the last step, is to lead the discussion without generating the content. Instructional techniques that can help facilitate the application of the learning include: (a) asking each person to identify how he or she will use this new information and generate a personal action plan; (b) asking like-interest groups to discuss common applications and share them with the large group; (c) asking partners to contract with one another about action items; and (d) conducting a role play using a real situation to practice newly learned techniques. The role play restarts the "discovery learning" process. Debrief afterward, revealing any additional concepts and discussing how to execute what has been practiced.

When you use this approach with experienced learners, that is, those for whom the knowledge and/or skill has been a part of their daily work for some time, such as coaching techniques for long-term supervisors, you may find that they move more quickly from the learning experience (Step 2) to Steps 4 and 5, unveil concepts and execute. Novice learners have a tendency to remain stuck in the learning experience and may have a difficult time recognizing the broader concepts and principles and their application. Thus, you must determine the experience level of the participants and be prepared to help those who are having difficulty moving on.

FACILITATOR EXPERTISE

Conducting effective experiential learning activities requires basic facilitation skills, such as how to ask and respond to questions and how to encourage dialogue and discussion. Complex learning objectives require more advanced facilitation skills, such as how to address conflict and how to recognize and customize for various learning styles. The same is true when participants will be learning about complex issues involving risk, motivation, resistance to change, and so on. In addition, facilitators must have presentation skills, such as recording information on a flip chart effectively and the ability to use other audiovisual equipment.

Conclusion

The experiential learning cycle, although acknowledged as important, is often forgotten or short-changed during training. The SEDUCE acronym will help any trainer or facilitator keep this important process in mind. The approach can be used to design and deliver content on any topic. SEDUCE *your* learners.

Lori L. Silverman, M.S., M.B.A., is the owner of Partners for Progress, a management consulting firm that helps organizations achieve and maintain a sustainable competitive advantage in the marketplace. She has a wide range of public- and private-sector management consulting experience in strategic management, large-scale organizational change, and total quality management.

Linda Ernst, R.N., B.A., M.S., is the president of Training Resource, an independently owned contract-training service. She facilitates workshops on management development, performance appraisal, interpersonal and business communications, and train-the-trainer for industrial and organizational clients. She is the co-author of Temperament and Type Dynamics: The Facilitator's Guide *(Temperment Research Institute).*

MAKING THE TRANSFER PROCESS WORK

Paul L. Garavaglia

Abstract: Training does not automatically result in increased productivity. An understanding of how what is learned in training is transferred can help to ensure the efficacy of training. The Transfer Design Model described here shows how the many elements that are included in and affect the transfer of training can be utilized to increase the application of knowledge and skills gained in training. The model also can be used as a diagnostic tool with which to assess existing training.

The components of the model are initial performance measures (quantified performance needs tied to business needs); systemic design factors (trainee characteristics and organizational characteristics); instructional design factors (presenting information, practicing skills, and assessing performance); the training (timing and training results); the maintenance system (motivation, the organization, the work environment, and teamwork); and the transfer performance measure (the players and the techniques). Each of these is described in detail, and suggestions are offered for integrating the elements of each component into an overall strategy and design for maximizing the transfer of training.

$\mathbf{A}$lthough a needs analysis may suggest that training is appropriate, too often a performance problem does not go away after training has been completed. Training and increased productivity do not necessarily go hand in hand. An understanding of the transfer of training can shed some light on this dilemma. The transfer process must work in order to increase organizational performance.

"Transfer of training" is the effective and continued application to trainees' jobs of the knowledge and skills gained in training. In theory, transfer of training sounds relatively simple, but in practice it is difficult to attain.

"Near" and "far" transfer are terms commonly used by HRD practitioners. Near transfer refers to trainees' ability to apply skills in contexts that are the *same* as those encountered in the training setting. Examples of near-transfer skills are logging on to a computer, filling out a shipping request, and baking a pie.

Far transfer occurs when trainees apply skills in contexts that are *different* from those encountered in training. Examples of far transfer include handling an employee with personal problems, negotiating a contract, and making a sale.

To ensure transfer, both the training materials and the organizational systems should have transfer techniques designed into them. The Transfer Design Model (Garavaglia, 1994, 1995a, 1995b, 1996a, 1996b) provides a comprehensive process for doing just that.

TRANSFER DESIGN MODEL

A good model depicts a process in a way that helps the user to think about, organize for, carry out, and even improve on the process. It shows the steps of the process in a way that makes parallel and sequential steps clear and indicates where feedback occurs. The Transfer Design Model is shown in Figure 1. It identifies the many elements that are included in, and therefore affect, a training program and offers an overall picture of the transfer process. The Transfer Design Model can be used to analyze and understand transfer problems in any organization and can provide aid in selecting appropriate interventions for solving those problems.

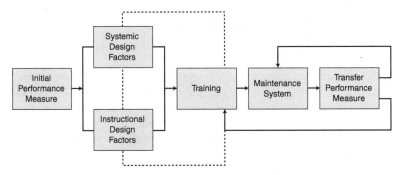

Figure 1. The Transfer Design Model

Initial Performance Measure

The process represented by the Transfer Design Model begins with an initial performance measure—the baseline performance measure that is targeted by the training. Without an initial performance measure, you may be trying to hit a target that does not exist. The initial performance measure should be obtained from needs-analysis data and then quantified and tied to business needs, problems, or opportunities.

Systemic Design Factors

The next two stages of the model, systemic design factors and instructional design factors, can be both concurrent and iterative. Systemic design factors are trainee characteristics and organizational characteristics. Any of these factors can create barriers to transfer, so they must be considered as part of the instructional management system.

Trainee Characteristics

Trainee characteristics consist of the affective attributes of trainees and the effect that they have on learning. These characteristics can be grouped into three categories: motivation, training, and the trainee. Emotions and attitudes that could adversely affect motivation and learning must be identified, challenged, and changed. For example, a group of participants may attend a training session with the attitude that they "don't need to be there." The trainer might challenge that attitude by asking questions and listening. Sometimes allowing participants to vent will change their attitudes. At other times the trainer may negotiate with the participant, asking that he or she give the session a try for a certain amount of time. And sometimes the trainer may have "proof," in the form of data, statistics, or actual articles that will help change participants' emotions or attitudes.

The trainee category includes the ways in which trainees approach goal setting related to the training. Bavetta, Gist, and Stevens (1990) found that people who are trained in self-management techniques that focus on goals and how to attain them have higher transfer and higher subsequent performance levels than do people who are trained in setting goals and what makes goals effective. Another aspect of the trainee category is the training overview that is presented at the beginning of the training session. An optimistic overview that states what the trainees are going to learn and be able to do at the end of training has a more positive impact on transfer than a realistic overview in which both positive and negative (e.g., the performance problem) information is relayed (Karl & Ungsrithong, 1992). Apparently, an overview that sounds pejorative or remedial is discouraging for trainees. In addition, the trainees' belief in the value of the training ("What's in it for me?") is important. If the trainees find the content invalid, they may transfer knowledge and skills that are inappropriate for effective job performance.

The trainee category includes how the ability level of the trainees affects transfer, the trainees' levels of self-efficacy (belief that one can execute a given task in a given setting), and their expectations regarding outcome (i.e., that a given outcome will occur if they engage in the behavior). The experiential background of the trainees also can help or hinder transfer. Richey (1992) found that the more education and training experience a trainee had, the greater the retention of knowledge after training.

Organizational Characteristics

Organizational characteristics that affect transfer include information obtained from interactions with supervisors and peers that affect a trainee's perception of reality regarding the organizational climate. These perceptions of the organizational climate, in turn, affect transfer. For example, if supervisors are unfamiliar with the training content and perceive it as having no value, they will be reluctant to allow their employees to attend training programs. This almost certainly eliminates any chance for the new skills to be applied on the job. Also, the supervisor's perception of the trainees' abilities affects the trainees' opportunity to perform new skills. Supervisors who have little confidence in their subordinates will not assign them challenging tasks in which new skills can be applied. This occurs despite the fact that the "enlightened" belief is that supervisors must prepare their employees for the challenges that the increasing complexity of work will bring.

Employees tend to model their supervisors' behaviors in order to gain rewards and recognition. If a supervisor behaves in ways that are congruent with the training objectives, the trainees will model that behavior, thus increasing the likelihood of transfer. Furthermore, support from peers can increase the likelihood of transfer, as can the pace of the work flow. If the work flow is fast, the trainees may believe that they are too busy to try new skills or they may think that using the new skills is the only way to achieve their goals. Either way, transfer is affected. If the pace of the work flow is too slow, the trainees may forget how to use their new skills.

Instructional Design Factors

While the instructional designers are creating training materials that take into account systemic design factors, they must also incorporate instructional design factors that will increase the likelihood of transfer. The Transfer Design Model includes a greater number of instructional design factors than do other similar models, specifically: presenting information, practicing skills, and assessing performance.

Presenting Information

When a trainer is presenting information, the use of examples can facilitate transfer. Multiple, varied examples allow the trainees to see skills or guidelines applied in different settings or circumstances. A good example of application can be contrasted to a bad example of application or an example of lack of application in order to clarify.

Analogies can be used to show how important concepts and principles apply in various situations. Analogies describe structural, functional, or causal similarities or differences between two things. Properly used analogies create a way for the trainee to tie new concepts and principles to old ones.

Principles are statements of cause-and-effect relationships that provide for action. Explaining the principles behind what a trainee is learning allows the trainee to bring more background to his or her attempt to use the new skills on the job. For example, a trainee should be taught principles of electricity, such as alternating and direct currents, before he or she is expected to connect a three-way electrical switch.

A packet given to the trainees prior to the actual training program can help to stress the relevance of the upcoming training. Such a packet should contain materials that link what the trainees already know to what they are about to learn, provide a preview of what is to be learned, and state organizational reasons for providing the training and possible benefits to the trainees.

Mnemonics can be used to create mental images to make instruction more meaningful. For example, to reinforce memory of the phases of an instructional design model, "ADDIE" can be used to help the trainees to remember analysis, design, development, implementation, and evaluation. Catchy phrases that have special meaning and specific numbering patterns also can be used as mnemonics.

Information displays (graphics, lists, etc.) are important in order to bring a visual element to the training. Information displays are used to draw attention and create perception; they mediate between the subject matter and the trainees. Several media are available for this purpose, including flip charts, overhead projectors, computers, posters, and videos. The more the information can be displayed visually, the better the subject matter will be learned by the trainees.

Allowing trainees the opportunity to explore training materials prior to attending the training has many benefits. These include allaying fears, arousing interest, and engendering positive feelings about the upcoming training. Training materials can be sent to the trainees in many formats, some of which include videotapes, audio cassettes, training manuals, and tips for getting the most out of the training.

Practicing Skills

A simulation is a model of a process or activity that approximates actual or operational conditions. Simulations can be used to make learning faster and safer by providing hands-on experience in controlled environments. If the trainees are to learn psychomotor and perceptual aspects of a task, a psychomotor-task simulation is appropriate. A cognitive-task simulation can be used to teach concepts and abstractions that underlie rules and principles. A verbal-task simulation, such as a role play, can be used when teaching communication and coordination skills. Finally, virtual reality can be used so that trainees can experience, interact with, and manipulate three-dimensional images.

Repetition and practice can also be used. Knowing when to use each is important because the proper practice technique can go a long way toward streamlining training and facilitating transfer. It is best to use repetition when critical stimulus elements do not vary. It is best to use practice when they do.

Assessing Performance

It is not enough to present information and have the trainees practice desired skills. Performance also must be assessed. Learner-driven and problem-centered techniques can be used in assessing performance. Such techniques replicate on-the-job conditions or are carried out on the job in order to allow the trainees to demonstrate that they can apply the desired knowledge or skills and produce desired outcomes in the work environment. For example, customer service representatives may be placed in the telephone queue to receive calls from customers. This provides the trainees with opportunities to demonstrate their knowledge and skills.

In action learning, work groups (usually between six and thirty employees and sometimes including vendors and/or customers) take an actual problem to the training session and are responsible for solving the problem. Trainees commit to an action plan and are held accountable for carrying out the plan. Assessment is based on the trainees' work in solving the problem (process) as well as the effectiveness of the plan (result). Action learning works best with trainees who are the "just do it" types.

Self-assessment may be the most effective type of assessment for some trainees. Learning outlines are self-assessments that identify what the trainees will start, stop, and keep doing as a result of the training, and how they will measure the success of each (stop, start, and keep doing).

Training

After the training materials are put together, the next stage of the model is the actual training. This is the stage in which "the rubber meets the road," and we begin to sense what effect the training will have on the original performance problem. In the Transfer Design Model, some training factors (goal setting versus self-management and realistic overview versus optimistic overview) are categorized as systemic design factors because they must be incorporated into the design of the training.

Timing

When the actual training takes place, in terms of the trainee's job context, supervisory support, organizational support, and personal life, can affect the trainees' ability to transfer knowledge and/or skills. Things to consider include the following:

- Will the organizational climate support the use of the new skills?
- Will the work flow allow for the use of new skills?
- Will follow-up training or support be available when the "training high" wears off?
- Are the trainees' personal or family stresses at an acceptable level?

Training Results

There are basically five outcomes (Baldwin & Ford, 1988) that can be obtained in regard to transfer:

1. The trainees transfer the desired skills initially and then taper off, slowly approaching the pre-training level;

2. The trainees fail to transfer skills, and the post-training level drops immediately after they return to the work site;

3. Trainees attempt to use the new skills on the job but, after a period of time, there is a sharp decline in the use of the skills, quickly approaching the pre-training level;

4. The trainees' learning and retention is minimal with little chance for transfer; and

5. The trainees' skill level increases over time after they are back on the job.

Both systemic and instructional design factors can determine whether skills are learned. The maintenance system (to be described) can affect whether and how skills are used on the job. Richey (1992) suggests that 20 to 45 percent of the variance in post-training behavior is because of design (systemic and instructional) factors. It is possible that the remaining 55 to 80 percent of the variance is because of factors in the maintenance system.

Maintenance System

Decisions should be made before the training begins about what systems, practices, and so on will be in place when the trainees return to the work setting in order to support and reinforce the desired behaviors. After training, the trainee goes back to the job and into a maintenance system that should promote the use of the newly acquired skills. Making the transfer of training succeed takes a concerted effort on the part of the trainees and their supervisors and/or managers. A robust maintenance system takes into account motivation, the organization, the work environment, and teamwork.

Motivation

Rewards and incentives can encourage the application of skills and knowledge gained in training. For this to occur, the use of skills and knowledge gained in training should be acknowledged and rewarded; nonuse should also be noted, but not rewarded. The application of skills and knowledge gained in training should not be discouraged or punished. Positive reinforcement helps to maintain the application of new skills and knowledge. Words of encouragement can be given "in process," while a trainee is working, or "post process," when the trainee has completed a task or project.

If a feedback loop is not established between trainees and their supervisors or managers, the transfer process can come to a halt. Feedback on performance can be formative or corrective (designed to correct or improve behavior) or maintaining or reinforcing (desired to acknowledge and maintain satisfactory performance) or passive (so as not to reinforce poor performance or in order to reinforce independent or entrepreneurial performance). Feedback also can be active (generally used to modify or correct poor performance or to acknowledge good performance). It is important to give feedback in an appropriate and timely manner and not to wait until something goes wrong. In other words, avoid the LAZY (leave alone/zap you) style of management.

The Organization

Obstacles are anything (or anyone) that prevents the skills and knowledge gained in training from being applied on the job. When obstacles are identified through the trainee/supervisor feedback loop or other evaluation efforts, they should be removed. Removal of obstacles helps to facilitate transfer.

Changes often must be made in the organization in order for transfer to succeed. Changes in the organization include changes made to the organizational structure (the functions of an organization and the reporting relationships) and changes made to the organizational system (how the work is done). Changes in the organizational structure include changes in the span of control or in the number of functions or subordinates a manager has and changes in organizational depth—the number of layers that exist between top and bottom levels of management, as well as layers between management and the workers. Changes in the organizational system are changes that focus on work processes. A well-defined work process can make the transition from the training program to the job much smoother by defining and structuring roles and responsibilities, empowering employees, and aligning work processes with the organization's values and culture.

The Work Environment

The work environment should be conducive to the use of new skills. Having the right equipment, tools, and materials to do the job is a must for streamlining the way work is done and increasing productivity. Ergonomics also should be considered. If employees develop sore backs or wrists from working at computers or if they are not able to reach some controls easily, they are likely to focus on these issues rather than on applying new skills. Ergonomic improvements can allow employees to concentrate on how they are doing the work, rather than on what happens to them (negatively) as a result of trying to do it.

Job aids can act as on-the-job cues for guiding performance. Job aids can reduce the amount of information that trainees must memorize. An additional benefit is that information can be accessed in real time, providing sufficient direction on how and when to perform a task. Job aids are particularly useful for tasks that are performed rarely, are very critical, or are highly complex, or when conditions or procedures change frequently or there is no time available for training. Job aids are not always appropriate, especially if the employees' hands and eyes are engaged in other activities, if people could lose credibility (e.g., with customers or suppliers) by using job aids, if employees do not have the skills to use the job aids, or if recalling needed information is a matter of life and death.

Teamwork

Booster sessions—meetings in which the trainees and trainer discuss the use of new skills on the job—and buddy systems in which trainees are paired off to reinforce one another and to maintain learning can increase the likelihood of transfer. The goal of each of these is to provide guidance for using new knowledge and skills, to maintain and encourage trainee learning, and to avoid relapse to pre-training levels of performance by keeping trainees motivated. In other words they should be GEMs: guiding, encouraging, and motivating.

Transfer Performance Measure

Ultimately, it is the measure of transfer performance that determines how successful the training was in correcting the original performance problem. This measure is often called Level Three evaluation (Kirkpatrick, cited in Michalak & Yager, 1979) and measures the effect the training had on the problem. For example, a glass manufacturer may want to reduce the amount of glass that is broken. Measures before and after the training could be used to show whether the training helped to correct the problem. The Transfer Design Model uses the transfer performance measure as the main pivot point for making decisions. If one compares the transfer performance measure to the initial performance measure and finds insufficient transfer, one can determine that the problem lies in the maintenance system or the training. If the problem is the training, it may be because of the systemic design or instructional design factors. Some of the reasons for obtaining a transfer performance measure are to ensure job security for trainers and designers by providing data to show that the training is effective, to show how training leads to organizational improvement, and to verify the soundness of the curriculum and maintenance systems.

Rationale

The transfer performance measure can determine how the training must be changed, what assistance the trainees need after they return to their jobs, and what prevents the trainees from applying what they learned in the training to their jobs. It also can measure the longevity of retention of a new skill by comparing performance at follow-up time with performance at the end of training. It is estimated that 40 percent of the skills learned are transferred immediately, 25 percent remain in use six months later, and 15 percent remain one year later. These measurements are based on the most common time frame for measuring transfer—six months—and the most common intervals—six-month or one-year intervals. When determining the timing of a transfer performance measure, allow the trainee enough time to use the new skills on the job.

The Players

Cost, bias, and time are the main criteria that affect a transfer performance measure. When determining who will actually measure the transfer, consider using internal training staff for existing programs and using professional evaluators for new training programs in order to avoid bias. Another possible way to avoid bias is to have a colleague of the designer of the training measure the transfer, if this person would be unbiased. Other likely candidates are instructors, trainees who create self-reports, line managers or supervisors, and external contractors. The best candidate may be different in different organizations because of the interplay of cost, bias, and time.

The Techniques

Measuring transfer is important in order to show management the value of a training program. When determining how to measure transfer, consider: (1) the cost of developing the method or instrument; (2) the types of skills and/or knowledge to be measured; (3) an acceptable response rate; and (4) how long it will take, if necessary, to train interviewers, observers, data collectors, and so on. Commonly used methods for measuring transfer are line-manager and supervisor reports, trainee self-reports, surveys or questionnaires, action plans, interviews, observation, qualification sessions, job simulations, and performance appraisal data—if the data is specific, accurate, and up-to-date.

Identifying the purpose of the transfer performance measure can help in determining which method to use. If the goal is to prove that the trainees actually learned something, collect evidence that the new skills and knowledge are being applied on the job. To diagnose the training effort, try to discover what helps and hinders transfer. To establish the merit of the training, collect pre- and post-training data on performance. To test the maintenance system, conduct assessments and interviews at regular intervals after training. To demonstrate performance improvement, focus on the change from the initial performance measure to the transfer performance measure. There may not be one "right" method for measuring transfer; each situation should be considered individually and the pros (benefits) and cons (time, expenses, effect in the organization, etc.) of each method should be reviewed. Once you know what you want to measure and the appropriate method, determine whom to obtain information from. The optimum audience to obtain information from is the total trainee group. However, the time and/or cost involved or other constraints can make surveying the total group unfeasible. In this case a sample of the total group can be used.

SUMMARY

Successful training involves two phases: the acquisition of skill or knowledge and the maintenance of desired behavior when the trainees return to the job. The Transfer Design Model attempts to facilitate successful training variables involved in the total training, transfer, maintenance, and measurement process. It pinpoints organizational systems that must be in place to support trainees after they return to the job. Such considerations may change the look and feel of training or radically change the organizational structure. The challenge for HRD practitioners is to learn how to better affect the transfer of training and, at the same time, to show how training can have a positive effect on the bottom line.

References

Baldwin, T.T., & Ford, K.J. (1988). Transfer of training: A review and directions for future research. *Personnel Psychology, 41*(1), 63–105.

Bavetta, A.G, Gist, M.E., & Stevens C.K. (1990). Transfer training method: Its influence on skill generalization, skill repetition, and performance level. *Personnel Psychology, 43*(3), 501–523.

Garavaglia, P.L. (1993). How to ensure transfer of training. *Training & Development, 47*(10), 63–68.

Garavaglia, P.L. (1994). *Transfer of training. . .guaranteed!* Proceedings of the 1994 World Productivity Assembly and Human Resource Development Asia Conference. Singapore: World Productivity Assembly at Human Resource Development Asia.

Garavaglia, P.L. (1995a). The ins and outs of transfer. *Performance and Instruction, 34*(5), 24–27.

Garavaglia, P.L. (1995b). *Transfer of training: Making training stick.* Info-Line 9512. Alexandria, VA: American Society for Training and Development.

Garavaglia, P.L. (1996a). Applying a transfer model to training. *Performance and Instruction, 35*(4), 4–8.

Garavaglia, P.L. (1996b). The transfer of training: A comprehensive process model. *Educational Technology, 36*(2), 61–63.

Karl, K.A., & Ungsrithong, D. (1992). Effects of optimistic versus realistic previews of training programs on self-reported transfer of training. *Human Resource Development Quarterly, 3*(4), 373–384.

Michalak, D.F., & Yager, E.G. (1979). *Making the training process work.* New York: Harper & Row.

Richey, R.C. (1992). *Designing instruction for the adult learner.* London: Kogan Page.

Paul L. Garavaglia *is a principal consultant with The ADDIE Group, Inc. He is the author of the book* Transfer of Training: Making Training Stick. *He is also a two-time winner of the American Society for Training and Development's Instructional Technology Blue Ribbon Award, once for the job aid "Making the Transfer Process Work" and again for the handbook* Managers as Transfer Agents. *Mr. Garavaglia has published transfer-related articles in* Corporate University Review, Educational Technology, Performance Improvement, *and* Training & Development.

CONTRIBUTORS

Kristin Arnold
Quality Process Consultants, Inc.
18 Jayne Lee Drive
Hampton, VA 23664-1545
(757) 850-4879
e-mail: QPCINC@aol.com

Philip Benham
Director, Graduate School HRMIR
Saint Francis College
Loretto, PA 15940-0600
(814) 472-3166
fax: (814) 472-3369
e-mail: pbenham@sfcpa.edu

Zane L. Berge, Ph.D.
Director, Training Systems
University of Maryland Baltimore
County
Department of Education
1000 Hilltop Circle
Baltimore, MD 21250
(410) 455-2306
fax: (410) 455-3986
e-mail: berge@umbc2.umbc.edu

Robert Alan Black, Ph.D.
RAB, Inc.
Creating People, Places & Possibilities
P.O. Box 5805
Athens, GA 30604
(706) 353-3387
fax: (706) 369-1400
e-mail: merrybeing@athens.net

Michael P. Bochenek, Ph.D.
Assistant Professor, Business
Administration
Elmhurst College
190 Prospect Avenue
Elmhurst, IL 60126
(630) 617-3119
fax: (630) 617-6497
e-mail: michaelb@elmhurst.edu

Brooke Broadbent
Broadbent Associates
867 Explorer Lane
Orleans, Ontario K1C2S3
Canada
(613) 837-6472
e-mail: brooke@mondenet.com
URL: www.brookebroadbent.
mondenet.com

Marlene Caroselli
Center for Professional Development
324 Latona Road, Suite 6B
Rochester, NY 14626-2714
(716) 227-6512
fax: (716) 227-6191
e-mail: mccpd@aol.com

Lisa De Diemar
5136 Polen Drive
Kettering, OH 45440
(937) 436-5748
e-mail: lisa_dediemar@ketthealth.
com.

Jeanne L. Engle
Goals Beyond Zero
P.O. Box 14144
Madison, WI 53714
(608) 222-2033

Linda Ernst
Training Resource
17382 Mayor Lane
Huntington Beach, CA 92647
(714) 847-5622
fax: (714) 842-9833
e-mail: trresource@aol.com

Julie Furst-Bowe
Communications, Education and
Training Department
University of Wisconsin-Stout
Menomonie, WI 54751
(715) 232-1321
fax: (715) 232-1441
e-mail: bowej@uwstout.edu

Paul L. Garavaglia
The ADDIE Group, Inc.
57 Dennison Street
Oxford, MI 48371
(248) 969-4920
fax: (248) 969-2342
e-mail: ADDIEGroup@aol.com

Peter R. Garber
210 Edelweiss Drive
Wexford, PA 15090
(412) 434-3417
fax: (412) 434-3490

Barbara Pate Glacel, Ph.D.
VIMA International
5290 Lyngate Court
Burke, VA 22015
(703) 764-0780
fax: (703) 764-0789
e-mail: BPGlacel@vima.com
URL: www.vima.com

Catherine Hayden
Hayden Carmichael Training
2724 Payne Street
Evanston, IL 60201
(847) 328-9308
fax: (847) 328-9312
e-mail: hctrain@interaccess.com

Herbert S. Kindler, Ph.D.
Center for Management Effectiveness
P.O. Box 1202
Pacific Palisades, CA 90272
(310) 459-6052
fax: (310) 459-9307
e-mail: kindlerCME@aol.com
URL: www.vima.com

Brian Korzec
Health Care Finance Administration
7500 Security Boulevard
Baltimore, MD 21244
(410) 786-6408
e-mail: BKORZEC@HCFA.GOV

Jean G. Lamkin, Ph.D.
Corporate Training Director
Landmark Communications, Inc.
150 W. Brambleton Avenue
Norfolk, VA 23510
(757) 446-2913
fax: (757) 446-2985
e-mail: jlamkin@lcimedia.com

Stanley L. Lamkin, Ph.D.
Senior Program Manager
Digital Equipment Corporation
6406 Ivy Lane
Greenbelt, MD 20770
  (301) 918-5776
  fax: (301) 918-7790
  e-mail: stanlamkin@digital.com

Gerald V. Miller, Ph.D.
President
Gerald V. Miller Associates
218 M Street, SW
Washington, DC 20024
  (202) 554-8334
  fax: (202) 554-8710
  e-mail: gvm@radix.net

Sherry R. Mills
Creative Training Associates
P.O. Box 25806
Colorado Springs, CO 80936
  (719) 380-1412
  fax: (719) 380-1412
  e-mail: fjctcm@aol.com

Mary Anne Newkirk
Changeworks
5352 Smooth Meadow Way, #1
Columbia, MD 21044
  (410) 997-3743
  fax: (410) 964-9893
  e-mail: manewkir@jagunet.com

Julie O'Mara
President
O'Mara and Associates
5979 Greenridge Road, Suite 100
Castro Valley, CA 94552-1817
  (510) 582-7744
  e-mail: omaraassoc@aol.com

Scott B. Parry
Training House, Inc.
P.O. Box 3090
Princeton, NJ 08543-3090
  (609) 452-1505
  fax: (609) 452-2790
  e-mail: TrngHouse@aol.com

John W. Peterson
Creative Training Associates
P.O. Box 25806
Colorado Springs, CO 80936
  (719) 380-1412
  fax: (719) 380-1412
  e-mail: fjctcm@aol.com

Robert C. Preziosi
Nova Southeastern University
3301 College Avenue
Ft. Lauderdale, FL 33316
  (954) 262-5111
  fax: (954) 262-3965

Emile A. Robert, Jr., Ph.D.
VIMA International
5290 Lyngate Court
Burke, VA 22015
  (703) 764-0780
  fax: (703) 764-0789
  e-mail: ChumRob@vima.com
  URL: www.vima.com

Beverly Robinson, Ph.D.
3876 Feedwire Road
Dayton, OH 45440
  (937) 848-8850
  e-mail: brobinson@desire.wright.edu

Dana Gaines Robinson
Partners in Change, Inc.
2547 Washington Road, Suite 720
Pittsburgh, PA 15241-2557
  (412) 854-5750
  fax: (412) 854-5801
  e-mail: PICinPGH@aol.com

James C. Robinson
Partners in Change, Inc.
2547 Washington Road, Suite 720
Pittsburgh, PA 15241-2557
  (412) 854-5750
  fax: (412) 854-5801
  e-mail: PICinPGH@aol.com

W. Kirk Roller, Ph.D.
1515 Jefferson Davis Highway,
  Suite 1405
Arlington, VA 22202
  (703) 416-6618
  e-mail: kroller225@aol.com

Lori L. Silverman, M.S., M.B.A.
Partners for Progress
2427 East 59th Court
Spokane, WA 99223-8904
  (509) 443-1320
  voice mail: (800) 253-6398
  fax: (509) 443-1620
  e-mail: pfprogress@aol.com

Taggart Smith, Ed.D.
1420 Knoy Hall of Technology
Purdue University
West Lafayette, IN 47907-1420
  (765) 494-6391
  e-mail: tesmith@tech.purdue.edu

Michael Stanleigh
Business Improvement Architects
85 Scarsdale Road, Suite 302
Toronto, Ontario M3B 2R2
Canada
  (416) 444-8225
  fax: (416) 444-6743
  e-mail: mcs@istar.ca

**Sivasailam "Thiagi" Thiagarajan,
  Ph.D.**
Workshops by Thiagi
4423 East Trailridge Road
Bloomington, IN 47408-9633
  (812) 332-1478
  fax: (812) 332-5701
  e-mail: thiagi@thiagi.com
  URL: www.thiagi.com

Jossey-Bass/Pfeiffer Annual Questionnaire

Place an X in the appropriate column, using the following scale to rate each item:

1=Very Little   2=Minimally   3=Somewhat   4=Moderately   5=Completely

Content	1	2	3	4	5
To what extent:					
Do you view the content as cutting edge?	—	—	—	—	—
Is the list of content areas complete and all-inclusive?	—	—	—	—	—
Is the level of activities appropriate for your needs?	—	—	—	—	—

Your Comments:
(other topics you'd like to see, etc.)

_____

_____

_____

Format	1	2	3	4	5
To what extent:					
Does the format allow you to locate general topics easily?	—	—	—	—	—
Does the format allow you to locate a specific activity or article quickly?	—	—	—	—	—
Is the writing tone and style appropriate for today's audience?	—	—	—	—	—
Are you interested in having the *Reference Guide to the Annual* online or on CD-ROM?	—	—	—	—	—
Are you interested in having the *Annual* activities, questionnaires, and resources online or on CD-ROM?	—	—	—	—	—

Your Comments:

_____

_____

_____

Why do you purchase the *Annual?*

_____

_____

_____

What topics would you like to have added? Who would you like to see as contributors to the *Annual?*

_____

_____

_____

What other suggestions do you have to improve the *Annual?*

_____

_____

_____

About You

How many years have you used the *Annual?* _____

What is your occupation/title? _____

Return to: The Annual
Jossey-Bass/Pfeiffer
350 Sansome Street
San Francisco, CA 94104-1342
Fax: (415) 433-1711

Contents of the Companion Volume, The 1999 Annual: Volume 2, Consulting

---

*See Experiential Learning Activities Categories, p. 7, for an explanation of the numbering system.
**Topic is "cutting edge."

Why you should become an *Annuals* Standing Order Customer

Your guaranteed benefits

Become a Standing Order Customer and enjoy the benefits: • get your *Annuals* every year as soon as they are available • get your *Annuals* every year at the lowest price • return any *Annuals* that you don't want and get a refund • become eligible for other special offers. For over 25 years, the *Annuals* have been *the* human resource development tool for practitioners everywhere.

Our promise to you

Each year the *Annuals* will contain a gold mine of tips and tools guaranteed to improve your organization. As a Standing Order Customer, you will receive the two-volume *Annuals* set each year—or, if you prefer, we can send you *Volume 1* or *Volume 2* alone—when they are hot off the press, at the lowest price we can offer.

Your obligations

Don't worry! It's EASY. You'll get the *Annuals* automatically each year, along with a bill. When you look at the *Annuals*, we're sure you'll want them. But if for whatever reason you're less than satisfied—return your *Annuals* and you won't owe us a dime.

Call toll-free today 800.274.4434
Fax toll-free today 800.569.0443

Join the group and enjoy super resources— and super savings!